England

A History Trivia Collection and Notable Figures – 500 Questions and Answers, Plus Stories of the Icons Who Shaped a Nation

Welcome Aboard, Check Out This Limited-Time Free Bonus!

Ahoy, reader! Welcome to the Ahoy Publications family, and thanks for snagging a copy of this book! Since you've chosen to join us on this journey, we'd like to offer you something special.

Check out the link below for a FREE e-book filled with delightful facts about American History.

But that's not all - you'll also have access to our exclusive email list with even more free e-books and insider knowledge. Well, what are ye waiting for? Click the link below to join and set sail toward exciting adventures in American History.

Access your bonus here
https://ahoypublications.com/
Or, Scan the QR code!

Table of Contents

PART 1: ENGLISH HISTORY TRIVIA 1

INTRODUCTION 3

PREHISTORIC ENGLAND 5

THE ROMANS IN ENGLAND (55 BCE–410 BCE) 11

EARLY MEDIEVAL ENGLAND (410 BCE–1066 CE) 18

MEDIEVAL ENGLAND AND THE NORMAN CONQUEST (1066–
1485) 26

THE TUDORS (1485–1603) 33

THE PROTESTANT REFORMATION IN ENGLAND (1517–1684) 40

THE STUART DYNASTY (1603–1714) 47

ENGLISH CIVIL WAR (1642–1651) 52

THE COMMONWEALTH OF ENGLAND (1649–1660) 56

THE AGE OF ENLIGHTENMENT IN ENGLAND (1685–1815) 61

THE GLORIOUS REVOLUTION IN ENGLAND (1688–1689) 66

THE GEORGIAN ERA IN ENGLISH HISTORY (1714–1837) 70

INDUSTRIAL REVOLUTION IN ENGLISH HISTORY (1760–1840) 76

VICTORIAN ERA (1837–1901) 82

THE BOER WARS AND ENGLAND IN SOUTH AFRICA (1899–
1902) 87

THE EDWARDIAN ERA (1901–1914) 92

WORLD WAR I IN ENGLISH HISTORY (1914–1918) 97

INTERWAR BRITAIN (1918–1939) 101

THE GENERAL STRIKE IN ENGLAND (1926) 107

THE GREAT DEPRESSION IN ENGLAND (1929–1939) 111

ENGLAND'S INVOLVEMENT IN WORLD WAR II (1939–1945) 115

THE BLITZ (1940–1941) 118

THE COLD WAR IN RELATION TO ENGLAND (1947–1991)..................122

THE CORONATION OF QUEEN ELIZABETH II (1953) 128

MARGARET THATCHER ERA (1979-1990) 131

THE MINERS' STRIKE (1984-1985) 136

THE GOOD FRIDAY AGREEMENT (1998) 140

MODERN BRITAIN (2000S-PRESENT) 144

CORONATION OF KING CHARLES III (2023) 151

CONCLUSION..................155

PART 2: NOTABLE FIGURES IN ENGLISH HISTORY 157

INTRODUCTION 159

CHAPTER 1: WILLIAM THE CONQUEROR AND HENRY II: FOUNDATIONS OF A NATION..................161

CHAPTER 2: THOMAS BECKET AND HENRY VIII: CHURCH, CROWN, AND CONFLICT..................172

CHAPTER 3: ELIZABETH I AND THE RISE OF ENGLISH NAVAL POWER..................181

CHAPTER 4: SHAKESPEARE AND MARLOWE: SHAPING THE ENGLISH LANGUAGE 190

CHAPTER 5: ISAAC NEWTON AND ROBERT HOOKE: UNRAVELING THE UNIVERSE..................199

CHAPTER 6: JOHN LOCKE AND WILLIAM WILBERFORCE: PHILOSOPHIES OF FREEDOM 209

CHAPTER 7: JAMES WATT AND GEORGE STEPHENSON: STEAM AND STEEL..................219

CHAPTER 8: CHARLES DICKENS AND FLORENCE NIGHTINGALE: REFORM AND COMPASSION 229

CHAPTER 9: LEADERSHIP THROUGH THE LENS OF WORLD WAR II..................238

CHAPTER 10: QUEEN ELIZABETH II AND THE BEATLES 247

CONCLUSION..................256

CHECK OUT ANOTHER BOOK IN THE SERIES 258

WELCOME ABOARD, CHECK OUT THIS LIMITED-TIME FREE BONUS!..................259

SOURCES AND ADDITIONAL REFERENCES 260

IMAGE SOURCES..................263

Part 1: English History Trivia

Unlock the Pivotal Moments and Intriguing Characters of English History with 500 Interactive Questions and Answers

Introduction

Throughout the centuries, England has been at the forefront of major historical events that have shaped not only its own destiny but also that of the entire world. From royal scandals and political upheavals to scientific breakthroughs and cultural revolutions, there is no shortage of captivating tales from this small yet mighty country. In this introduction, we invite you to join us on a journey through time as we unlock some of the most pivotal moments and characters in English history. But unlike your typical history lesson, we will be exploring these stories in a fun and interactive way—through trivia questions!

Our collection includes 500 thought-provoking questions that cover various periods in English history. These questions are designed for kids but can be enjoyed by all ages. They are perfect for family game nights or educational activities in schools.

So why should you care about English history? Well, for one thing, it is full of enough drama and intrigue to rival any Hollywood blockbuster. From bloody battles between kings to secret affairs between queens, the stories of English history are filled with scandal and excitement. But beyond the entertaining aspects, studying history allows us to learn from past mistakes and understand how they have shaped our present.

Our trivia questions cover a wide range of topics, including monarchs, famous battles, important inventions and discoveries, cultural movements, and more. By answering these questions, you will not only expand your knowledge of English history but also gain insights into its impact on the world we live in today. But this is not just about testing your historical knowledge—it's about discovering lesser-known facts that may surprise even the most avid history buff. Did you know that Queen Victoria was an excellent pianist? Or that King Henry VIII had six wives? Through our trivia questions, you will discover fascinating details about influential figures such as William the Conqueror and Margaret Thatcher, while learning about events like the Miners' Strike or The Blitz.

So, whether you are a history enthusiast or just looking for some fun facts to impress your friends, our English history trivia book has something for everyone. We hope that this journey through time will not only pique your interest in English history but also inspire you to delve deeper into its rich and complex past. So, grab a pen and paper, gather your family or friends, and let's dive into the world of English history trivia!

Prehistoric England

This chapter will explore the fascinating history of prehistoric England. Discover how people lived during this period with limited resources and developed complex trade networks between themselves and neighboring nations! Gain insight into the lives of our prehistoric ancestors and find out what life was like before written records were kept in Britain.

1. What type of animal is commonly associated with prehistoric England?

    A. Woolly mammoth

    B. Saber-toothed tiger

    C. Wooly rhinoceros

    D. Giant sloth

2. What became the primary source of food for Britain during the Late Neolithic period?

    A. Hunting and gathering

    B. Farming and herding livestock

    C. Trading for food supplies

    D. Fishing in the ocean

3. Why was Stonehenge built during the prehistoric period?

    A. To create a sacred space for religious rituals

    B. For burials or memorials

    C. As defensive structures against invading armies

    D. To mark important astronomical events

4. What type of material were prehistoric tools made from?

    A. Iron

    B. Bronze

    C. Stone

    D. None of the above

5. What was the name of the land bridge that joined Britain to Europe ca. 14,000 years ago?

    A. Britannia

    B. Doggerland

    C. Pangea

    D. None of the above

6. Which of these statements is true about prehistoric Britain?

    A. A land bridge never existed between Britain and Ireland

    B. Britain was colonized by immigrants from southern Italy

    C. We know who built Stonehenge

    D. All of the above

7. When did the construction of Stonehenge begin according to archeologists?

    A. Fifth century BCE

    B. Late fourth millennium BCE

    C. 6000 BCE

    D. None of the above

8. What type of animal was domesticated in prehistoric England?

    A. Wolves

    B. Cats

    C. Sheep

    D. Elephants

9. Stonehenge is considered which of these?

    A. Monolith

    B. Cist

    C. Dolmen

    D. Megalith

10. What type of people are believed to have built Stonehenge?

  A. The Celts

  B. The Saxons

  C. The Druids

  D. We don't know

11. How did early farmers in Britain improve their agricultural techniques during the Neolithic period?

  A. By developing irrigation systems

  B. By advancing their tools

  C. By introducing new crops from other regions

  D. By using fertilizers to increase crop yields

12. What were the members of the ancient priestly class in Britain called?

  A. Druids

  B. Magi

  C. Rabbi

  D. Brahmins

13. Around when did Britain become part of the Atlantic trade system?

  A. 2000 BCE

  B. 1700 BCE

  C. 1300 BCE

  D. 600 BCE

14. What did early farmers in Britain use to plow their fields?

  A. Horses

  B. Donkeys

  C. Oxen

  D. Sheep

15. Which culture rose to prominence in Western Europe during the Late Bronze Age?

  A. Frankish

  B. Roman

  C. Celtic

  D. British

16. With which other region was Britain most culturally alike in the first millennium BCE?

A. Greece

B. France

C. Italy

D. Scythia

17. Western European societies during the Late Bronze Age are placed under which predominant archeological culture?

A. Hallstatt culture

B. Funnelbeaker culture

C. Clovis culture

D. None of the above

18. When did Iron Age begin in Britain?

A. 1000 BCE

B. 800 BCE

C. 500 BCE

D. 300 BCE

19. Which of these is considered one of the main archeological pieces of ancient Celtic art found in Britain?

A. Rosetta Stone

B. Battersea Shield

C. Sutton Hoo Helmet

D. None of the above

20. What event is typically considered the end of the British Iron Age?

A. Anglo-Saxon migration

B. Roman invasion

C. Late Iron Age collapse

D. British Civil War

21. Which of the following Iron Age buildings are found in large numbers in Britain?

A. Hillforts

B. Mastabas

C. Pyramids

D. Starforts

22. Which of these ancient historians first mentions Britain in his writings?

    A. Pytheas of Massalia

    B. Thucydides

    C. Diodorus Siculus

    D. Livy

23. Which of these tribes is thought to have invaded Britain ca. 300 BCE?

    A. The Boii

    B. The Galatians

    C. The Parisii

    D. The Danes

24. What is the oppidum?

    A. An early English legal code

    B. A large, fortified Iron Age settlement

    C. A type of temple found in Scotland

    D. None of the above

25. What year is the Snettisham Hoard dated to?

    A. 150 BCE

    B. 100 BCE

    C. 70 BCE

    D. 30 BCE

Answers

1. A. Woolly mammoth
2. B. Farming and herding livestock
3. D. To mark important astronomical events
4. C. Stone
5. B. Doggerland
6. A. A land bridge never existed between Britain and Ireland
7. B. Late fourth millennium BCE
8. C. Sheep
9. D. Megalith
10. D. We don't know
11. B. By advancing their tools
12. A. Druids
13. C. 1300 BCE
14. C. Oxen
15. C. Celtic
16. B. France
17. A. Hallstatt culture
18. B. 800 BCE
19. B. Battersea Shield
20. B. Roman invasion
21. A. Hillforts
22. A. Pytheas of Massalia
23. C. The Parisii
24. B. A large, fortified Iron Age settlement
25. C. 70 BCE

The Romans in England (55 BCE–410 BCE)

This chapter will explore the history of the Romans in England. We will discover how they brought significant economic, political, and social change to the region during their occupation, which lasted for almost five centuries. We'll explore how their presence influenced all aspects of life in England and look at some of the most important figures from this period.

26. What was the Roman province of Britain called?

    A. Britannia

    B. Romania

    C. Provincia Romana

    D. Britannicus

27. What did the Romans call the native Britons?

    A. Saxons

    B. Kalends

    C. Celts

    D. Picts

28. What is the name of the bridge originally built by the Romans across the River Thames?

    A. Boudicca Bridge

    B. Hadrian's Bridge

    C. Tower Bridge

    D. London Bridge

29. How many times did Julius Caesar invade Britain?

A. Once

B. Twice

C. Three times

D. Four times

30. When was the first Roman invasion of Britain organized?

A. 63 CE

B. 59 BCE

C. 55 BCE

D. 49 BCE

31. When was the conquest of Britain concluded?

A. 43 CE

B. 31 BCE

C. 65 CE

D. None of the above

32. Why is the *Commentarii de Bello Gallico* significant in regard to British and English history?

A. It is considered the earliest written document about British history

B. It was written by an unknown early British king

C. It contains the earliest mention of Britain in a foreign source

D. None of the above

33. Who is the author of the *Commentarii de Bello Gallico*?

A. Bede

B. Livy

C. Thucydides

D. Julius Caesar

34. What was the outcome of the Boudican uprising?

A. Total Roman defeat

B. Roman retreat from Britain

C. A failed attempt at liberating Britain from Roman rule

D. None of the above

35. When did the Boudican revolt take place?

A. 26-27 CE

B. 60-61 CE

C. 75-76 CE

D. 103-104 CE

36. Who was Boudica?

A. The claimant to the British throne

B. The legendary ancestor of King Arthur

C. The warrior-queen of the Britons

D. The Roman general who joined the Britons

37. Which of these Roman emperors constructed a defensive fortification in northern Britain to mark the extent of Roman rule?

A. Claudius

B. Nero

C. Theodosius

D. Hadrian

38. Who fought against the Romans during their conquest of Britain?

A. The Picts

B. The Celts

C. The Belgae

D. All of the above

39. What was the main export of early Roman Britain?

A. Agricultural products

B. Metals

C. Pottery

D. None of the above

40. Which of these was the earliest capital of Roman Britain?

A. York

B. Colchester

C. Caernarvon

D. London

41. What became Britain's biggest port when the Romans were there?

    A. Dover

    B. London

    C. Bristol

    D. Colchester

42. What were the civitas?

    A. Administrative divisions of Roman Britain

    B. The court system of Roman Britain

    C. Governor's personal bodyguards in Roman Britain

    D. Both a and b

43. What caused the end of Roman rule in Britain?

    A. Invasions of the Angles and Saxons

    B. Worsening relations with Rome

    C. Internal revolt

    D. All of the above

44. Approximately how many people lived in Roman Britain by the late third century, during the peak of Roman rule?

    A. one million

    B. two million

    C. three million

    D. five million

45. Who is considered the first British Christian martyr?

    A. St. Nicholas

    B. St. Alban

    C. St. George

    D. None of the above

46. What language did most of the British population speak on an everyday basis during Roman rule in Britain?

    A. Latin

    B. Angle

    C. Brittonic

    D. Celtic

47. Which Roman general expanded Roman rule in Britain as far north as Caledonia?

A. Tacitus

B. Agricola

C. Gnaeus

D. Gracchus

48. Which of these emperors reformed the administrative structure of Britain during their reign in 197 CE?

A. Claudius

B. Marcus Aurelius

C. Trajan

D. Septimius Severus

49. Which emperor introduced the office of the *vicarius* to Britain with his administrative reforms?

A. Justinian

B. Diocletian

C. Antoninus Pius

D. Caracalla

50. What was the responsibility of a *vicarius*?

A. He was the supreme justice of the province

B. He was the most important official in the province

C. He was the deputy military chief of the province

D. None of the above

51. What did Emperor Antoninus Pius do to try to keep the Picts out of Roman Britain?

A. Built a wall

B. Offered a trade deal

C. Established centers of exchange on the border

D. None of the above

52. When did Rome withdraw from Britain?

A. 400 CE

B. 405 CE

C. 407 CE

D. 410 CE

53. What was the main problem Rome experienced in Britain during the fourth and early fifth centuries?

A. A series of rebellions

B. The migration of northern tribes into the south

C. A ten-year plague

D. None of the above

54. Where was most of the Roman influence concentrated in Britain?

A. West

B. Southwest

C. Center and east

D. North

55. Which Roman emperor may have declined to send assistance to Britain in the early fifth century?

A. Honorius

B. Arcadius

C. Theodosius

D. Constantius

Answers

26. A. Britannia
27. C. Celts
28. D. London Bridge
29. B. Twice
30. C. 55 BCE
31. A. 43 CE
32. A. It is considered the earliest written document about British history
33. D. Julius Caesar
34. C. A failed attempt at liberating Britain from Roman rule
35. B. 60-61 CE
36. C. The warrior-queen of the Britons
37. D. Hadrian
38. D. All of the above
39. B. Metals
40. B. Colchester
41. B. London
42. A. Administrative divisions in Roman Britain
43. D. All of the above
44. C. three million
45. B. St. Albam
46. C. Brittonic
47. B. Agricola
48. D. Septimius Severus
49. B. Diocletian
50. B. He was the most important official in the province
51. A. Built a wall
52. D. 410 CE
53. A. A series of rebellions
54. C. Center and east
55. A. Honorius

Early Medieval England (410 BCE–1066 CE)

In the early medieval period of 410 BCE–1066 CE, England experienced many changes. People left their small villages for new towns or cities and built castles to protect them. Kings became powerful rulers, and Christianity started to spread. Peasants tilled the soil, farmers kept their herds, and merchants and traders traveled far and wide. It was a fascinating time full of new experiences and discoveries!

56. What type of government existed in early medieval England?

A. Monarchy

B. Communism

C. Democracy

D. Autocracy

57. In what year did William the Conqueror become the ruler of England?

A. 1040 CE

B. 1100 CE

C. 1066 CE

D. 1085 CE

58. How many battles were fought by Alfred the Great during his campaign in 871?

   A. 5

   B. 7

   C. 3

   D. 9

59. From where did the Anglo-Saxons primarily migrate to England?

   A. Western France

   B. Northern Germany and the Low Countries

   C. Northern Iberia

   D. Western Scandinavia

60. What language did the population of England start to speak after the Anglo-Saxon migration?

   A. Old English

   B. Late Brittonic

   C. Latin

   D. Middle English

61. Who began to increasingly invade England from the late eighth century?

   A. The Franks

   B. The Vikings

   C. The Irish

   D. The Spanish

62. Which famous English king issued The Great Charter, or Magna Carta, in 1215 CE?

   A. Alfred the Great

   B. William I

   C. Henry II

   D. John

63. Who was the first Anglo-Saxon king to convert to Christianity according to the *Ecclesiastical History of the English People?*

    A. Alfred the Great

    B. Æthelbert of Kent

    C. Edward the Confessor

    D. Henry I

64. How many kingdoms did the Anglo-Saxon migrants eventually establish in England?

    A. 3

    B. 4

    C. 6

    D. 7

65. How are the Anglo-Saxon kingdoms of early Middle Ages England commonly referred to?

    A. Heptarchy

    B. Pentarchy

    C. Triarchy

    D. None of the above

66. Which of these was an Anglo-Saxon kingdom?

    A. Wessex

    B. Kent

    C. East Anglia

    D. All of the above

67. In what year did the Battle of Hastings take place?

    A. 1041 CE

    B. 1066 CE

    C. 1086 CE

    D. 1100 CE

68. King Penda was a prominent ruler of which of these Anglo-Saxon kingdoms?

    A. Northumbria

    B. Wessex

    C. Mercia

    D. Kent

69. When year did the "Great Heathen Army" invade England?

    A. 865 CE

    B. 870 CE

    C. 878 CE

    D. 881 CE

70. Who led the English against the Vikings at the Battle of Edington?

    A. Alfred the Great

    B. William the Conqueror

    C. Edward the Confessor

    D. Æthelbert

71. Which monastery did the Vikings attack in 793?

    A. Kent

    B. Lindisfarne

    C. York

    D. Lincoln

72. Until when did Alfred the Great rule England?

    A. 865 CE

    B. 886 CE

    C. 889 CE

    D. 899 CE

73. What was the name of the tribute paid to the Vikings by the Englishmen?

    A. Burh

    B. Scandpenny

    C. Danegeld

    D. None of the above

74. What was the name of the king who ruler Denmark, Norway, and England until his death in 1035?

    A. Æthelbert of Kent

    B. Cnut the Great

    C. Harald Hardrada

    D. William the Conqueror

75. Which English city became the center of the Danish presence in England in 867?

A. Kent

B. York

C. Lincoln

D. Stratfordshire

76. Which Viking managed to conquer and become the king of England for five weeks in 1013?

A. Cnut the Great

B. Thorkell

C. Sweyn Forkbeard

D. Gurthu

77. Who was the author of the famous work *Ecclesiastical History of the English People?*

A. Alfred the Great

B. Monke Nene

C. The Venerable Bede

D. None of the above

78. Which of the Anglo-Saxon kingdoms managed to unite England in 927?

A. Northumbria

B. East Anglia

C. Mercia

D. Wessex

79. Who became the first ing of the English in 927?

A. Edward the Confessor

B. Alfred the Great

C. Æthelstan

D. Offa

80. Who emerged victorious from the Battle of Stamford Bridge in 1066?

A. Harald Hardrada

B. Harold Godwinson

C. Neither side

D. None of the above

81. Where was William I crowned the king of England?

A. Westminster Abbey

B. The Tower of London

C. Buckingham Palace

D. St. Paul's Cathedral

82. What was the name of the manuscript produced by William the Conqueror after the survey of the English population in the late eleventh century?

A. The Norman Cofex

B. The Great Charter

C. The Domesday Book

D. None of the above

83. Under which of these kings did the Kingdom of Mercia reach the height of its power?

A. Offa

B. Ceolred

C. Peada

D. Eowa

84. Who was the last crowned king of England before the invasion of William the Conqueror?

A. Edward the Confessor

B. Harold Godwinson

C. Harald Hardrada

D. Ecbert

85. Who succeeded Alfred the Great on the throne of England after his death?

A. Æthelstan

B. Edward the Elder

C. Edgar

D. Eadred

Answers

56. A. Monarchy
57. C. 1066 CE
58. D. 9
59. B. Northern Germany and the Low Countries
60. A. Old English
61. B. The Vikings
62. D. John
63. B. Æthelbert of Kent
64. D. 7
65. A. Heptarchy
66. D. All of the above
67. B. 1066 CE
68. C. Mercia
69. A. 865 CE
70. A. Alfred the Great
71. B. Lindisfarne
72. D. 899 CE
73. C. Danegeld
74. B. Cnut the Great
75. B. York
76. C. Sweyn Forkbeard
77. C. The Venerable Bede
78. D. Wessex
79. C. Æthelstan
80. B. Harold Godwinson
81. A. Westminster Abbey
82. C. The Domesday Book
83. A. Offa
84. B. Harold Godwinson
85. B. Edward the Elder

Medieval England and the Norman Conquest (1066–1485)

In 1066, England began a period known as the Middle Ages, which lasted more than 400 years. Medieval England was a time of castles, knights, and grand feasts. Kings and queens reigned, and battles were fought on the plains and in the cities. Lords and ladies gathered in the court to discuss important matters. People lived in small towns and villages and traveled on dirt roads. Join us as we uncover the secrets of medieval England—a fascinating time when history was made.

86. Who fought in the Battle of Hastings?

    A. The English and the French

    B. The Danes and the Swedes

    C. The Normans and the Saxons

    D. The Scots and the Irish

87. How was the English social system organized during the Middle Ages?

    A. It was a theocracy

    B. It was a merchant oligarchy

    C. It was a feudal monarchy

    D. It was a republic

88. What religion did most people in medieval England practice?

A. Judaism

B. Christianity

C. Islam

D. Pagan

89. Who was king of England from 1066-1087?

A. Henry I

B. William the Conqueror

C. John I

D. Richard I

90. On what day was William the Conqueror crowned as king?

A. May 14

B. October 13

C. December 25

D. January 1

91. What is the name of a series of campaigns waged by the Normans after the conquest in northern England to deal with local rebellions?

A. Harrying of the North

B. Massacre of Northumbria

C. The Northern Crusade

D. None of the above

92. What was the Magna Carta?

A. A charter of trade rules

B. A document setting out the rights and privileges of the church

C. A treaty between the pope and the kings of England

D. An agreement between the king and the barons of England, setting out basic rights

93. What formal title did William hold before conquering England?

A. Count

B. Duke

C. King

D. Lord

94. Who inherited the kingdom after the death of William the Conqueror?

A. William II

B. Robert

C. James I

D. John I

95. In medieval England, how was someone declared an outlaw?

A. By sentence of an ecclesiastical court

B. By fleeing the kingdom

C. By declaring bankruptcy

D. By sentence of a feudal court

96. What is the period of English history between 1138 and 1153 also known as?

A. The Time of Troubles

B. The Anarchy

C. The First Civil War

D. The Crisis

97. Who was the first of the Angevin rulers of England?

A. Robert

B. Stephen de Blois

C. Henry I

D. Henry II

98. Which of these kings inherited the French provinces of Anjou and Normandy and later acquired Aquitaine through marriage?

A. Henry II

B. Richard I

C. Henry III

D. George I

99. Which house formed the short-lived Angevin Empire, which included territories of England and France in the twelfth and the thirteenth centuries?

A. Westminster

B. Normans

C. Plantagenets

D. Stuarts

100. Which English king participated in the Third Crusade?

A. John I

B. Henry II

C. Richard I

D. Richard II

101. Which of these English kings managed to lose many of the French possessions?

A. Eleanor of Aquitaine

B. John I

C. Richard I

D. Richard III

102. Which of these English kings was captured by Simon de Montfort during the Second Barons' War in 1264?

A. Richard II

B. Edward I

C. Henry III

D. Henry IV

103. What did guilds mainly do in the Middle Ages?

A. Contributed funds to the church

B. Set labor standards and wages

C. Lend money to the royal family

D. None of the above

104. Who defeated Simon de Montfort at the Battle of Evesham?

A. Edward I

B. Henry III

C. Roger Mortimer

D. Edward II

105. What year is considered the beginning of the Hundred Years' War between England and France?

    A. 1330

    B. 1337

    C. 1339

    D. 1341

106. Why did the Hundred Years' War break out?

    A. Edward III was assassinated by the French

    B. French nobles wanted to undermine the English monarchy

    C. Edward III claimed the French throne

    D. All of the above

107. Who did Edward the Black Prince capture in 1356, after the Battle of Poitiers?

    A. His father, Edward III

    B. King John II of France

    C. Chateau Josselin

    D. None of the above

108. At which battle did the English decisively defeat the French in 1415?

    A. Calais

    B. Orleans

    C. Agincourt

    D. Rouen

109. What was the main strength of the English army during the medieval period?

    A. Heavy cavalry

    B. Innovative artillery

    C. Pikemen

    D. Longbowmen

110. Who emerged victorious from the Hundred Years' War?

    A. England

    B. France

    C. Neither side

    D. We don't know

111. Which English king was deposed in 1399?

    A. Richard II

    B. Richard III

    C. Henry IV

    D. Henry V

112. How are the series of civil wars in England that began in 1455 referred to?

    A. The Game of Thrones

    B. The Wars of the Claimants

    C. The Wars of the Roses

    D. The Struggles of the Yorks

113. Who was the king when the civil war began?

    A. Henry IV

    B. Henry V

    C. Henry VI

    D. Henry VII

114. What was one of the main reasons for England's instability in the mid-fifteenth century?

    A. A new plague

    B. Economic problems caused by the Hundred Years' War

    C. Unstable line of succession in the House of Plantagenet

    D. Riots in London and York

115. Which two cadet houses of the House of Plantagenet vied for power at the beginning of the civil war?

    A. Tudor and Hannover

    B. York and Hannover

    C. Westminster and Tudor

    D. York and Lancaster

Answers

86. C. The Normans and the Saxons
87. C. It was a feudal monarchy
88. B. Christianity
89. B. William the Conqueror
90. C. December 25
91. A. Harrying of the North
92. D. An agreement between the king and the barons of England, setting out basic rights
93. B. Duke
94. A. William II
95. D. By sentence of a feudal court
96. B. The Anarchy
97. D. Henry II
98. A. Henry II
99. C. Plantagenets
100. C. Richard I
101. B. John I
102. C. Henry III
103. B. Set labor standards and wages
104. A. Edward I
105. B. 1337
106. C. Edward III claimed the French throne
107. B. King John II of France
108. C. Agincourt
109. D. Longbowmen
110. B. France
111. A. Richard II
112. C. The Wars of the Roses
113. C. Henry VI
114. B. Economic problems caused by the Hundred Years' War
115. D. York and Lancaster

The Tudors (1485–1603)

Four hundred years ago was a time of revolution in England. This period is known as the Tudor period. It began with the coronation of King Henry VII in 1485 and continued until Queen Elizabeth I's death in 1603. During this time, the Tudors changed England forever, creating a powerful and unified nation. Grand palaces were built, explorers discovered new lands, and books were printed for the first time. It was a time of adventure and intrigue filled with examples of bravery, ambition, power, and love. In this chapter, dive into the era of the Tudors and discover England's way of life during this period.

116. Which English king had six wives?

A. Henry VIII

B. Edward VII

C. George III

D. Charles I

117. The Tudors were descendants of a noble family from which kingdom?

A. England

B. Ireland

C. Spain

D. Wales

118. Who was the founder of the Tudor dynasty?

    A. Edward VI

    B. Henry VII

    C. Charles I

    D. George III

119. Which English king signed the Treaty of Troyes—an agreement during the Hundred Years' War that would have made him inherit the throne of France?

    A. Henry V

    B. Edward VI

    C. Henry VI

    D. John II

120. When did the War of the Roses end?

    A. 1479

    B. 1480

    C. 1485

    D. 1487

121. Who took the throne after Elizabeth I, ending the Tudor dynasty?

    A. James I

    B. Edward VI

    C. Charles I

    D. Henry VII

122. Who managed to briefly seize power in England before being defeated by Henry VII?

    A. Henry VI

    B. Richard III

    C. Charles I

    D. Oliver Cromwell

123. What was the last significant battle of the War of the Roses?

    A. Agincourt

    B. Deorham

    C. Brunanburh

    D. Bosworth Field

124. With which European kingdom did England forge an alliance in the fourteenth century that lasted for hundreds of years and is still ongoing?

A. Spain

B. Portugal

C. Poland

D. Italy

125. Who were the parents of Elizabeth I?

A. Henry VIII and Anne Boleyn

B. Edward VI and Jane Seymour

C. Henry VII and Catherine Parr

D. Charles I and Anne Boleyn

126. How did Elizabeth I earn the nickname "The Virgin Queen"?

A. By refusing to marry

B. By staying in her castle

C. By joining a convent

D. By wearing white dresses

127. When did Henry VII die?

A. 1505

B. 1507

C. 1509

D. 1511

128. The Act of Supremacy declared the English sovereign to be the supreme head of what?

A. The Church of England

B. The Catholic Church

C. The British Empire

D. The British Parliament

129. The Church of England was created by which English king?

A. Henry VIII

B. Henry IX

C. Charles I

D. Charles II

130. **Over what Christian doctrine did the English Reformation initially break with Catholicism?**

    A. Prohibition of adultery

    B. Prohibition of divorce

    C. Prohibition of alcohol

    D. Prohibition of priestly marriage

131. **Who was executed for treason in 1536?**

    A. Mary Queen of Scots

    B. Lady Jane Grey

    C. Elizabeth I

    D. Anne Boleyn

132. **Which monarch reversed many of the Protestant policies of their predecessors after rising to the throne of England in 1553?**

    A. Elizabeth I

    B. Mary I

    C. Edward VI

    D. Charles I

133. **Who succeeded the throne of England in 1547 after the death of Henry VIII?**

    A. Edward V

    B. Henry IX

    C. Edward VI

    D. Elizabeth I

134. **Which kingdom's king did Mary marry in 1556?**

    A. Portugal

    B. Spain

    C. France

    D. Denmark

135. **Who came to the throne after the death of Mary I?**

    A. Elizabeth I

    B. Charles I

    C. John II

    D. Edward VII

136. **How were Elizabeth I and Mary, Queen of Scots, related?**

A. They were sisters

B. They were mother and daughter

C. They were cousins

D. They were not related

137. **The Elizabethan period coincided with which major artistic movement?**

A. Baroque

B. Classical

C. Gothic

D. Renaissance

138. **What was one of the main achievements of Elizabeth I's reign?**

A. Expansion into France

B. End of domestic religious conflicts

C. Development of trade with China

D. Reformation of the Parliament

139. **With which nation did England go to war during the late 1580s?**

A. Portugal

B. Spain

C. France

D. Denmark

140. **When did the Spanish Armada attack England?**

A. 1569

B. 1588

C. 1590

D. 1591

141. **The defeat of the Spanish Armada resulted in what?**

A. The English becoming independent

B. The recognition of England as a major European power

C. A rise in trade with other countries

D. Catherine of Aragon becoming queen of England

142. Who was the last Tudor monarch?

    A. Mary Tudor

    B. Edward VI

    C. Elizabeth I

    D. Henry VIII

143. Which admiral led the English forces in defeating the Spanish Armada?

    A. Ralph Dalaval

    B. John Paveley

    C. Francis Drake

    D. None of the above

144. When did Elizabeth I die?

    A. 1600

    B. 1602

    C. 1603

    D. 1605

145. What treaty ended the Anglo-Spanish War?

    A. The Peace of Tilsit

    B. The Treaty of London

    C. The Peace of Dover

    D. The Treaty of Madrid

Answers

116. A. Henry VIII
117. D. Wales
118. B. Henry VII
119. A. Henry V
120. C. 1485
121. A. James I
122. B. Richard III
123. D. Bosworth Field
124. B. Portugal
125. A. Henry VIII and Anne Boleyn
126. A. By refusing to marry
127. C. 1509
128. A. The Church of England
129. A. Henry VIII
130. B. Prohibition of divorce
131. D. Anne Boleyn
132. B. Mary I
133. C. Edward VI
134. B. Spain
135. A. Elizabeth I
136. C. They were cousins
137. D. Renaissance
138. B. End of domestic religious conflicts
139. B. Spain
140. B. 1588
141. B. The recognition of England as a major European power
142. C. Elizabeth I
143. C. Francis Drake
144. C. 1603
145. B. The Treaty of London

The Protestant Reformation in England (1517–1684)

The Protestant Reformation began in Germany in 1517 and quickly reached England. This movement had an enormous impact on politics, religion, and culture during this period. Protestants challenged traditional beliefs about God, faith, and worship, leading to changes in how people practiced their faith. The English monarchy also changed this era, with rulers like Henry VIII introducing new religious practices into the country. By 1684, the Protestant Reformation had ended, but it left behind a legacy still seen today!

146. **What event marked the beginning of the Protestant Reformation?**

   A. Martin Luther's 95 Theses

   B. King Henry VIII's divorce from Catherine of Aragon

   C. Queen Elizabeth I's ascension to the throne

   D. John Wycliffe's translation of the Bible into English

147. **Who was considered the leader of the Protestant Reformation in England?**

   A. Jan Hus

   B. Thomas Cranmer

   C. John Calvin

   D. King James I

148. **Which king founded the Anglican Church?**

    A. Henry VII

    B. Henry VIII

    C. Edward VI

    D. Elizabeth I

149. **Which of these was part of the Act of Uniformity?**

    A. To provide equal rights to Catholics and Protestants

    B. To create a single, unified church among Catholics and Protestants

    C. To establish an English Bible in every parish

    D. To require everyone to attend mass weekly

150. **How did the Puritans view religious ceremonies?**

    A. They believed them to be necessary for salvation

    B. They felt they should be done with as much pomp and ceremony as possible

    C. They only approved of simple, meaningful rituals

    D. They rejected all religious ceremonies

151. **What were some long-term consequences of the Protestant Reformation in England?**

    A. Increased economic prosperity

    B. Forced conversion to Catholicism

    C. Burning of Bibles

    D. Increased power for Roman Catholic priests

152. **What was the purpose of William Laud's policies?**

    A. To restore divine order

    B. To increase royal control over church matters

    C. To reduce restrictions on nonbelievers

    D. To promote toleration between Catholics and Protestants

153. **Which organization was formed to move away from the Church of England?**

    A. The Congregationalists

    B. The Quakers

    C. The Anglicans

    D. The Puritans

154. Who wrote *The Pilgrim's Progress,* one of the most influential works during the Protestant Reformation in England?

A. Thomas More

B. John Bunyan

C. William Tyndale

D. Martin Luther

155. How did Queen Elizabeth I respond to religious differences within her kingdom?

A. She executed anyone who challenged her authority

B. She allowed freedom of worship but imposed restrictions on any religion that threatened her rule

C. She tried to mediate between the Church of England and Roman Catholics

D. None of the above

156. What did the Test Act of 1673 require?

A. That all citizens be tested for literacy

B. That all citizens take a loyalty oath to the Church of England

C. That all Roman Catholics pay an additional tax

D. That only Anglicans could hold public office

157. What was the "High Church" during The Protestant Reformation in England?

A. A church where services were held in Latin and conducted by priests wearing elaborate vestments

B. A church that focused on treating Protestants like second-class citizens

C. An emphasis on strict orthodoxy, religious ritualism, and episcopal government

D. An effort to move away from hierarchical authority structures within the Church of England

158. Under which ruler was the prominence of Roman Catholicism briefly restored in England?

A. Mary I

B. Elizabeth I

C. Edward VI

D. Oliver Cromwell

159. What did the Toleration Act of 1689 allow for during the Protestant Reformation in England?

A. Non-Anglicans to hold public office

B. Conversion from Catholicism to Anglicanism

C. Religious freedom for all denominations except Catholics

D. Freedom of worship within certain limits

160. Under King James I, which Christian denomination did Scotland mostly adhere to?

A. Protestantism

B. Catholicism

C. Orthodoxy

D. Methodism

161. What was the significance of the Thirty-nine Articles?

A. To proclaim spiritual independence from Rome

B. To serve as a declaration of faith for Anglicans

C. To provide equal rights to Catholics and Protestants

D. To create a single, unified church

162. How did King Charles I respond to religious differences within his kingdom?

A. He tried to impose uniformity on all denominations

B. He allowed freedom of worship but imposed restrictions on any religion that threatened his rule

C. He abolished the Church of England

D. He promoted toleration for all religious denominations

163. Who wrote *The Book of Common Prayer* during the Protestant Reformation in England?

A. Thomas Cranmer

B. John Wycliffe

C. William Tyndale

D. Martin Luther

164. **What did the Elizabethan Settlement accomplish during the Protestant Reformation in England?**

A. It required everyone to attend mass weekly

B. It established an English Bible in every parish

C. It created a single, unified church

D. It established tolerance of different religious beliefs

165. **What was the purpose of John Calvin's teachings during the Protestant Reformation in England?**

A. To promote a return to Catholic orthodoxy

B. To increase royal control over Church matters

C. To restore divine order

D. To emphasize humans' responsibility for their own salvation

166. **Who led one of the most influential movements toward reform within the Church of England and became archbishop of Canterbury in 1533?**

A. William Tyndale

B. Martin Luther

C. John Wycliffe

D. Thomas Cranmer

167. **What was the purpose of King James I's King James Bible during the Protestant Reformation in England?**

A. To promote tolerance between Catholics and Protestants

B. To have a new version of the Bible in English

C. To tax those who did not adhere to Protestantism

D. None of the above

168. **Who were the Recusants in England during the Reformation?**

A. Followers of Elizabeth

B. An underground extreme Protestant group

C. Roman Catholics who refused to attend mandatory services of the Anglican Church

D. None of the above

169. How did most Catholic priests and bishops initially respond to Puritan efforts?

A. They supported them wholeheartedly

B. They tolerated their presence but disagreed with their views

C. They persecuted Puritan views

D. They tried to mediate between different denominations

170. Who wrote the *Institutes of The Christian Religion*?

A. William Tyndale

B. John Bunyan

C. Martin Luther

D. John Calvin

Answers

146. A. Martin Luther's 95 Theses

147. B. Thomas Cranmer

148. B. Henry VIII

149. C. To establish an English Bible in every parish

150. C. They only approved of simple, meaningful rituals

151. A. Increased economic prosperity

152. B. To increase royal control over church matters

153. D. The Puritans

154. B. John Bunyan

155. B. She allowed freedom of worship but imposed restrictions on any religion that threatened her rule

156. D. That only Anglicans could hold public office

157. C. An emphasis on strict orthodoxy, religious ritualism, and episcopal government

158. A. Mary I

159. D. Freedom of worship within certain limits

160. A. Protestantism

161. B. To serve as a declaration of faith for Anglicans

162. A. He tried to impose uniformity on all denominations

163. A. Thomas Cranmer

164. D. It established tolerance of different religious beliefs

165. D. To emphasize humans' responsibility for their own salvation

166. D. Thomas Cranmer

167. B. To have a new version of the Bible in English

168. C. Roman Catholics who refused to attend mandatory services of the Anglican Church

169. C. They persecuted Puritan views

170. D. John Calvin

The Stuart Dynasty (1603–1714)

The Stuart dynasty resided over an exciting period in British history. It came to power in England when King James VI of Scotland became King James I of England in 1603, uniting the two countries and creating what is now known as Great Britain. For the next 111 years, members of this powerful family ruled England, Scotland, and Ireland. They brought a wealth of knowledge from their Scottish homeland and used it to create new laws that favored all people regardless of class or background. This period also witnessed notable advances in science, literature, and art!

171. **When was the Stuart dynasty founded?**

    A. 1594

    B. 1603

    C. 1371

    D. 1714

172. **What religion were most of the Stuarts?**

    A. Protestant

    B. Catholic

    C. Christian

    D. Jewish

173. What happened to King Charles I during his reign as leader?

A. He abdicated

B. He was exiled

C. He was executed

D. He died in battle

174. When did Queen Anne become ruler of England, Scotland, and Ireland?

A. 1603

B. 1702

C. 1714

D. 1688

175. Who was the last monarch in the Stuart dynasty?

A. James II

B. Queen Anne

C. Charles I

D. Elizabeth I

176. What event caused King James II to be removed from power?

A. The Glorious Revolution

B. Gunpowder Plot

C. War of Spanish Succession

D. English Civil War

177. How many children did Mary, Queen of Scots, have?

A. 1

B. 2

C. 3

D. 4

178. Which religion was favored by King Charles I?

A. Protestantism

B. Catholicism

C. Baptism

D. Judaism

179. Where did Prince Charles Edward Stuart die?

    A. London

    B. Scotland

    C. France

    D. Italy

180. Which of these rulers ascended the throne in 1660?

    A. James I

    B. Charles II

    C. Elizabeth I

    D. Mary, Queen of Scots

181. What did King Charles I do to start a civil war?

    A. He tried to diminish the role of the Parliament

    B. He wanted to invade Spain

    C. He raised taxes

    D. He imposed religious reforms

182. When did The English Bill of Rights take place?

    A. 1603

    B. 1702

    C. 1688/9

    D. 1714

183. Who defeated James II at Battle of Boyne in Ireland?

    A. William III

    B. George III

    C. Anne

    D. James IV

184. Where did the Battle of Boyle take place?

    A. Scotland

    B. The Netherlands

    C. England

    D. Ireland

185. **Why did the English nobility dislike James II?**

    A. He had abolished the Parliament

    B. He had been a Catholic

    C. He had raised their taxes

    D. None of the above

186. **Who was Mary, Queen of Scots' son?**

    A. Charles I

    B. Charles II

    C. James VI and I

    D. Henry VIII

187. **When did the English Civil War begin?**

    A. 1633

    B. 1642

    C. 1649

    D. 1645

188. **When did William and Mary take the throne?**

    A. 1603

    B. 1702

    C. 1714

    D. 1688

189. **Who was the last Catholic monarch of England?**

    A. Charles II

    B. Charles I

    C. James VI and I

    D. Mary II

190. **Who was the oldest son of James I and Anne of Denmark?**

    A. George III

    B. William of Orange

    C. Henry Frederick

    D. Mary, Queen of Scots

Answers

171. C. 1371
172. B. Catholic
173. C. He was executed
174. B. 1702
175. B. Queen Anne
176. A. The Glorious Revolution
177. A. 1
178. B. Catholicism
179. D. Italy
180. B. Charles II
181. A. He tried to diminish the role of the Parliament
182. C. 1688/9
183. A. William III
184. D. Ireland
185. B. He had been a Catholic
186. C. James VI and I
187. B. 1642
188. D. 1688
189. C. James VI and I
190. C. Henry Frederick

English Civil War (1642–1651)

The English Civil War was a time of great unrest in England. Between 1642 and 1651, two groups fought against each other: the Royalists, who wanted to keep the king in power, and the Parliamentarians, who wanted more rights for ordinary people. Both sides used powerful weapons like cannons and muskets as they battled on land and at sea. In the end, the Parliamentarians won, but not without paying a heavy price—many lives were lost during this devastating war!

191. What caused the English Civil War?

    A. A disagreement between King Charles I and Parliament

    B. A battle fought between England and Scotland

    C. An argument among members of Parliament about religion

    D. None of the above

192. Which side was victorious in the English Civil War?

    A. The Royalists led by King Charles I

    B. The Roundheads led by Oliver Cromwell

    C. Neither—it ended in a draw

    D. The Scots under William Wallace

193. Who wrote "The Leveller Manifesto" during the English Civil War?

    A. Thomas Hobbes

    B. John Lilburne

    C. James Harrington

    D. William Penn

194. What years are referred to as the "Personal Rule" of Charles I?

    A. 1625-1628

    B. 1630-1648

    C. 1629-1640

    D. 1640-1648

195. Who was the father of Charles I?

    A. James VI and I

    B. James VII and II

    C. Henry VIII

    D. None of the above

196. Who was the leader of the Royalists during the English Civil War?

    A. Oliver Cromwell

    B. Charles I

    C. Henry VIII

    D. None of the above

197. What kind of government did Oliver Cromwell set up after winning the war?

    A. A constitutional monarchy

    B. An absolute monarchy

    C. A republic based on religious principles

    D. A protectorate with a range of executive powers

198. When did the Battle of Marston Moor take place?

    A. 1640

    B. 1641

    C. 1642

    D. 1644

199. Who emerged victorious from the Battle of Naseby?

    A. Charles I

    B. Cromwell

    C. Prince William

    D. Neither side

200. What was the name of the standing force established by the Parliamentarians during the First Civil War?

A. Army for Freedom

B. Liberty Corps

C. New Model Army

D. None of the above

201. When did the second stage of the English Civil War begin?

A. 1650

B. 1644

C. 1648

D. None of the above

202. What was the charge against Charles I that led to his execution?

A. Mismanagement of royal treasury

B. Treason

C. Regicide

D. Heresy

203. When did the Anglo-Scottish War begin?

A. 1649

B. 1650

C. 1651

D. 1652

204. When did the Parliamentarian army achieve victory over the Royalists at the battle of Preston?

A. 1648

B. 1642

C. 1549

D. 1776

205. What year did King Charles I surrender to Scottish forces and start negotiations for a peace treaty with the Roundheads?

A. 1645

B. 1647

C. 1649

D. None of these

Answers

191. A. A disagreement between King Charles I and Parliament
192. B. The Roundheads led by Oliver Cromwell
193. B. John Lilburne
194. C. 1629-1640
195. A. James VI and I
196. B. Charles I
197. D. A protectorate with a range of executive powers
198. D. 1644
199. B. Cromwell
200. C. New Model Army
201. C. 1648
202. B. Treason
203. B. 1650
204. A. 1648
205. B. 1647

The Commonwealth of England (1649–1660)

The Commonwealth of England was a period in British history from 1649 to 1660. It began when King Charles I was overthrown and the government changed to rule without a king or queen. During this era, England worked hard for peace and prosperity, laying foundations that still shape life today. People had new opportunities to express themselves through trade, religious freedom, literature, and art!

206. What was the Commonwealth of England?

    A. A constitutional monarchy

    B. A republic led by Oliver Cromwell

    C. An oligarchy

    D. All of the above

207. Why did the English government decide to create the Commonwealth of England?

    A. To restore the monarchy

    B. To stabilize after the civil war

    C. To increase trade

    D. To overthrow Parliament

208. **What was abolished during the Commonwealth of England?**

A. Monarchy

B. Religion

C. Slavery

D. All of the above

209. **How did Oliver Cromwell's rule differ from that of previous rulers in England?**

A. He increased taxes for all citizens

B. He implemented strict religious laws

C. He created more freedom and liberty than before

D. He brought temporary peace and unity among the people

210. **What kind of structure did Oliver Cromwell's government most resemble during the Commonwealth?**

A. Absolute monarchy

B. Constitutional monarchy

C. Parliamentary democracy

D. Military rule

211. **What religion was favored in the Commonwealth?**

A. Catholicism

B. Judaism

C. Protestantism

D. Islam

212. **What was Oliver Cromwell's title during the Commonwealth?**

A. Prime Minister

B. King

C. President

D. Lord Protector

213. **Who succeeded Oliver Cromwell as leader of England following his death in 1658?**

A. Richard Cromwell

B. James II

C. William III and Mary II

D. Elizabeth I

214. How were laws enforced by the government during the Commonwealth period?

A. With strict punishments

B. With negotiation and compromise

C. Through religious laws

D. With the help of local militias

215. What effect did the Commonwealth have on the economy of England?

A. It weakened it

B. It strengthened it

C. It had no impact

D. It caused inflation

216. How many lord protectors were there for the duration of the Commonwealth?

A. One

B. Two

C. Three

D. Four

217. Which of the following statements is true?

A. The Commonwealth diminished the authority of the king

B. The Commonwealth helped decrease taxes on the commoners

C. The Commonwealth managed to expand in England's colonies

D. The Commonwealth was ultimately a great success

218. What happened in 1660?

A. Oliver Cromwell died

B. The Commonwealth was attacked by France

C. Monarchy was restored

D. None of the above

219. Who was crowned king in Westminster Abbey in April 1661?

A. James VIII

B. Charles II

C. Richard Cromwell

D. William III

220. When was the Declaration of Breda issued?

A. April 1660

B. December 1660

C. May 1659

D. March 1658

Answers

206. B. A republic led by Oliver Cromwell

207. B. To stabilize after the civil war

208. A. Monarchy

209. D. He brought temporary peace and unity among the people

210. C. Parliamentary democracy

211. C. Protestantism

212. D. Lord Protector

213. A. Richard Cromwell

214. B. With negotiation and compromise

215. B. It strengthened it

216. D. Four

217. A. The Commonwealth diminished the authority of the king

218. C. Monarchy was restored

219. B. Charles II

220. A. April 1660

The Age of Enlightenment in England (1685–1815)

The Age of Enlightenment in England was a period from the late seventeenth to the mid-nineteenth century. It was when many people questioned traditional beliefs and began to think more critically about the world around them. During this era, famous philosophers such as John Locke, Isaac Newton, and David Hume helped bring revolutionary ideas to light that changed how we look at the world today!

221. Which major movement immediately preceded the Age of Enlightenment?

A. The Renaissance

B. The Scientific Revolution

C. The Industrial Revolution

D. The Age of Discovery

222. Which of these philosophers was influential during the Age of Enlightenment in England?

A. John Locke

B. Voltaire

C. Karl Marx

D. Thomas Hobbes

223. **Why did some people refer to this period as "the Age of Reason"?**

   A. Because it was a time when science and logic were used to solve social problems

   B. Because religious beliefs had been abolished

   C. Because political systems had changed significantly

   D. Because social conventions were relaxed

224. **Who wrote the widely read book *An Essay Concerning Human Understanding*?**

   A. John Locke

   B. Thomas Hobbes

   C. Voltaire

   D. Karl Marx

225. **Which country is considered the birthplace of the Age of Enlightenment?**

   A. England

   B. France

   C. Germany

   D. Italy

226. **Which of these is a purpose of the scientific method greatly developed during the Enlightenment?**

   A. To disprove theories

   B. To refute arguments

   C. To create hypotheses

   D. All of the above

227. **Which of these philosophers are known as the "social contract" theorists?**

   A. Jean-Jacques Rousseau

   B. John Locke

   C. Thomas Hobbes

   D. All of the above

228. Who is considered the "Father of Capitalism" and a leading Scottish scholar from the Enlightenment?

A. Thomas Hobbes

B. Adam Smith

C. Karl Marx

D. Jean-Jacques Rousseau

229. Who is the author of *Leviathan*?

A. Adam Smith

B. John Locke

C. Thomas Hobbes

D. Jean-Jacques Rousseau

230. What new ideas emerged during the Age of Enlightenment?

A. Capitalism

B. Socialism

C. Liberalism

D. All of the above

231. Which of these was not the main focus of early Enlightenment thinkers?

A. Social reform

B. Political change

C. Religious toleration

D. Emancipation of slaves

232. Which English thinker produced *The History of the Decline and Fall of the Roman Empire*?

A. Thomas Hobbes

B. John Locke

C. Edward Gibbon

D. Anthony Collins

233. Who wrote *On Liberty*?

A. John Stuart Mill

B. Adam Smith

C. Oliver Cromwell

D. Voltaire

234. What metaphorical significance does the Leviathan carry in *Leviathan*?

A. God

B. All-powerful ruler

C. Strongest warrior

D. Supreme military general

235. What were the public meeting places during the Enlightenment called in England?

A. Salons

B. Forums

C. Coffeehouses

D. Agora

Answers

221. B. The Scientific Revolution
222. A. John Locke
223. A. Because it was a time when science and logic were used to solve social problems
224. A. John Locke
225. B. France
226. D. All of the above
227. D. All of the above
228. B. Adam Smith
229. C. Thomas Hobbes
230. D. All of the above
231. D. Emancipation of slaves
232. C. Edward Gibbon
233. A. John Stuart Mill
234. B. All-powerful ruler
235. C. Coffeehouses

The Glorious Revolution in England (1688–1689)

The Glorious Revolution of 1688-1689 was a notable event in England's history. King James II was replaced by his daughter Mary and her husband William, who were invited to take the throne as joint rulers. This changed the balance of power between Parliament and the monarchy forever! The revolution also brought religious freedom to England, allowing people to practice their faith without fear of persecution or punishment.

236. What caused the Glorious Revolution in England?

A. A disagreement over taxes

B. Dissatisfaction with the monarchy

C. King James II's Catholic sympathies

D. All of the above

237. How did William and Mary become rulers during the Glorious Revolution?

A. By declaring war against England

B. They were elected by the people

C. King James appointed them as his successors

D. Through a series of deals with the nobility and the Parliament

238. **What was the nationality of William of Orange?**

A. English

B. Danish

C. Dutch

D. French

239. **How did the Glorious Revolution affect English politics?**

A. It gave more power to the nobles

B. It created an absolute monarchy

C. Parliament gained more power

D. None of the above

240. **What was one result of the Glorious Revolution in England?**

A. A decrease in religious violence

B. An increase in taxes

C. The end of freedom of religion

D. All of the above

241. **What was the "Bill of Rights"?**

A. A document that granted King James II more power

B. An agreement between William and Mary about how they would rule together

C. A list of rights for English citizens that limited the powers of kings and queens

D. None of the above

242. **What religion did Mary, the daughter of King James II, follow?**

A. Islam

B. Protestantism

C. Judaism

D. Catholicism

243. **What happened to King James II after the Glorious Revolution?**

A. He was executed for treason

B. He was reincorporated into English political life

C. He was forced to go into exile

D. None of the above

244. Who was the main political rival of William III in Europe?

A. Louis XIV

B. Louis XV

C. Charles V

D. William IV

245. How did the Glorious Revolution affect English citizens?

A. It gave them greater religious freedoms

B. It increased their taxes

C. It weakened their civil liberties

D. None of the above

Answers

236. D. All of the above
237. D. Through a series of deals with the nobility and the Parliament
238. C. Dutch
239. C. Parliament gained more power
240. A. a decrease in religious violence
241. C. A list of rights for English citizens that limited the powers of kings and queens
242. B. Protestantism
243. C. He was forced to go into exile
244. A. Louis XIV
245. A. It gave them greater religious freedoms

The Georgian Era in English History (1714–1837)

The Georgian period in English history was a time of notable change. During this era, the country experienced advances in science and technology, an expanding economy, and increased overseas exploration. The Georgians were also known for their love of fashion, art, and culture. This exciting time saw a blossoming of new ideas that helped shape Britain into the modern nation it is today!

246. The period of English history known as the Georgian era is named after which royal family?

    A. House of York

    B. House of Stuart

    C. House of Windsor

    D. House of Hanover

247. What event marked the end of the Georgian era in England?

    A. Industrial Revolution

    B. Great Fire of London

    C. Battle of Waterloo

    D. Accession of Queen Victoria to the throne

248. Which important legal document was adopted in the 1830s by the Georgian rulers of England?

A. Bill of Rights

B. Magna Carta

C. Royal Proclamation

D. Slavery Abolition Act

249. What was the official religion of England during the Georgian era?

A. Protestantism

B. Catholicism

C. Atheism

D. Anglicanism

250. Who founded the British Museum, an institution that still stands today?

A. Prince Albert

B. William Pitt

C. Lord Liverpool

D. Sir Hans Sloane

251. Which was the major political rival of Great Britain during this time?

A. France

B. Sweden

C. Austria

D. Russia

252. Which of these important developments originated during the Georgian era?

A. Colonization

B. Industrialization

C. Imperialism

D. None of the above

253. Which Protestant denomination gained a lot of following during this period?

A. Baptist Church

B. Evangelicalism

C. Presbyterianism

D. Puritanism

254. Who was the first prime minister of England during the Georgian era?

A. William Pitt

B. Lord North

C. Robert Walpole

D. Charles Grey

255. Which economic policy became popular in Britain during the Georgian era?

A. Capitalism

B. Socialism

C. Mercantilism

D. Communism

256. Which Scottish thinker is the author of *A Treatise of Human Nature*?

A. David Hume

B. John Locke

C. John Milton

D. Adam Ferguson

257. Under which king did England lose control of the Thirteen Colonies?

A. George IV

B. George V

C. George VI

D. George III

258. Who wrote *Gulliver's Travels,* one of the most popular works from the Georgian era?

A. Jonathan Swift

B. Jane Austen

C. Charles Dickens

D. Robert Burns

259. Which of these statements is true about the Georgian period in English history?

A. The Georgian era was relatively unimportant in English history

B. The Georgian era was marked by great social upheaval that destabilized the nation for generations

C. The Georgian era was instrumental in helping Great Britain become a global power

D. The Georgian era is considered the Golden Age of British history

260. What was an important economic factor during this period in English history?

A. Expansion of trade

B. Introduction of capitalism

C. Increase in French tariffs

D. Social welfare policies

261. Which architectural style became popular among wealthy citizens during the Georgian era?

A. Baroque

B. Gothic

C. Neoclassical

D. Victorian

262. Which of these conflicts were not fought during the Georgian era?

A. Seven Years' War

B. Thirty Years' War

C. Napoleonic Wars

D. American Revolutionary War

263. Which famous book, which is still widely read today, was published in England during the Georgian era?

A. *Frankenstein*

B. *Wuthering Heights*

C. *Pride and Prejudice*

D. *Robinson Crusoe*

264. Which playwright wrote *The School for Scandal*, a popular theatrical production of the era?

A. William Shakespeare

B. George Bernard Shaw

C. John Gay

D. Richard Brinsley Sheridan

265. Which important economic document was agreed upon by Great Britain during the Georgian era?

A. Common Market Agreement

B. Bretton Woods Agreement

C. Magna Carta

D. Navigation Acts

Answers

246. D. House of Hanover

247. D. Accession of Queen Victoria to the throne

248. D. Slavery Abolition Act

249. D. Anglicanism

250. D. Sir Hans Sloane

251. A. France

252. B. Industrialization

253. B. Evangelicalism

254. C. Robert Walpole

255. C. Mercantilism

256. A. David Hume

257. D. George III

258. A. Jonathan Swift

259. C. The Georgian era was instrumental in helping Great Britain become a global power

260. A. Expansion of trade

261. C. Neoclassical

262. B. Thirty Years' War

263. D. *Robinson Crusoe*

264. D. Richard Brinsley Sheridan

265. D. Navigation Acts

Industrial Revolution in English History (1760–1840)

The Industrial Revolution was a period of notable change in English history from 1760 to 1840. During this time, new inventions and ideas transformed how people worked and lived. Machines replaced manual labor, allowing production levels to skyrocket. Factories were built across England. People moved to cities for work opportunities, and wealth grew rapidly. This exciting time changed our lives forever. Who knew what amazing things would come next?

266. What is considered the main catalyst behind the Industrial Revolution?

    A. Technological inventions that accelerated the rate of production

    B. Policies of the British government after the loss of the Thirteen Colonies

    C. Peace agreement between Britain and France in 1815

    D. Building canals and expanding trade networks

267. During what century did most countries experience their Industrial Revolution?

    A. Eighteenth century

    B. Nineteenth century

    C. Twentieth century

    D. Twenty-first century

268. Which of these figures is considered instrumental in the development of the spinning frame?

A. William Wilberforce

B. Adam Smith

C. Richard Arkwright

D. Robert Owen

269. What type of industry experienced the greatest increase in production during the Industrial Revolution?

A. Textiles

B. Iron and Steel

C. Mining

D. Automotive

270. Which of these figures is credited with the invention of the steam engine?

A. Robert Owen

B. James Watt

C. Edmund Cartwright

D. None of the above

271. What was one result of industrialization in England?

A. Increased poverty of the masses

B. Overthrow of the monarchy

C. No major change

D. Increased production and wealth

272. How did new transportation improvements help cause the Industrial Revolution?

A. By increasing access to resources

B. By creating more efficient shipping routes

C. By making it easier for workers to travel

D. All of the above

273. Which instrument is not typically credited with increasing productivity during the Industrial Revolution?

A. Spinning wheel

B. Steam engine

C. Power loom

D. Printing press

274. Which of these was not an immediate negative effect of the Industrial Revolution?

A. Decreased wages

B. Increased class disparity

C. Environmental damage

D. More job opportunities

275. The problems created by the Industrial Revolution would be criticized by which major thinker of the nineteenth century?

A. John Stuart Mill

B. Abraham Lincoln

C. Karl Marx

D. Friedrich Hegel

276. What type of organization emerged during the Industrial Revolution that allowed skilled workers to negotiate with employers and achieve higher wages?

A. Labor unions

B. Guilds

C. Corporations

D. None of the above

277. What invention managed to regulate the speed of the steam engine that ultimately increased production?

A. Railways

B. Coal chute

C. Spinning jennies

D. Watt's governor

278. **Which of these was not an effect of the Industrial Revolution?**

A. A decrease in England's population

B. Expansion of the kingdom's colonial holdings

C. Rise of workers' rights movements

D. An increase in overall trade

279. **How did new inventions such as spinning jennies and power looms revolutionize the textile industry?**

A. Allowed for mass production

B. Increased labor costs

C. Reduced quality of the products

D. None of the above

280. **What major occurrence preceded the Industrial Revolution and was important in bringing it about?**

A. The Bill of Rights

B. Increase in Britain's agricultural production

C. The end of the Napoleonic Wars

D. None of the above

281. **What was the effect of the Industrial Revolution on demographic patterns?**

A. More people started to emigrate to Asia

B. Increased national mortality rate

C. Large-scale urban growth

D. All of the above

282. **Who is credited with the invention of the spinning jenny?**

A. Lewis Paul

B. James Watt

C. Daniel Bourn

D. James Hargreaves

283. **When was the spinning jenny invented?**

A. 1760

B. 1764

C. 1768

D. 1772

284. What energy source was used increasingly during this period, allowing for improved steam engine efficiency?

A. Water power

B. Petroleum

C. Coal

D. Solar power

285. What did the Reform Act of 1832 do?

A. Increase wages

B. Create a democracy

C. End slavery

D. Expand voting rights

Answers

266. A. Technological inventions that accelerated the rate of production

267. B. Nineteenth century

268. C. Richard Arkwright

269. A. Textiles

270. B. James Watt

271. D. Increased production and wealth

272. D. All of the above

273. D. Printing press

274. C. Environmental damage

275. C. Karl Marx

276. A. Labor unions

277. D. Watt's governor

278. A. A decrease in England's population

279. A. Allowed for mass production

280. B. Increase in Britain's agricultural production

281. C. Large-scale urban growth

282. D. James Hargreaves

283. B. 1764

284. C. Coal

285. D. Expand voting rights

Victorian Era (1837–1901)

Welcome to the Victorian Era, an exciting time in history! This period, which stretched from 1837 to 1901, was named after Queen Victoria. During this time, new inventions were created, including the telephone, typewriter, and light bulb. People also traveled around the world more than ever before. Explorers discovered new lands filled with exotic plants and animals. Fashion changed drastically during this era as well. Men wore suits with top hats, while women dressed in big hoop skirts over multiple layers of petticoats!

286. **What type of government did England have during the Victorian era?**

    A. A constitutional monarchy

    B. A socialist state

    C. An absolute monarchy

    D. A democratic republic

287. **When did the Great Exhibition take place in London, England?**

    A. 1851

    B. 1900

    C. 1837

    D. 1901

288. **What invention made transportation easier and faster for people during this period?**

A. Airplanes

B. Automobile

C. Trains

D. Hot air balloons

289. **When did Queen Victoria succeed the throne?**

A. 1870

B. 1873

C. 1875

D. 1877

290. **What caused a rise in industrialization during the Victorian era?**

A. Increased trade with foreign countries

B. Expansion of transportation networks

C. Development of new technologies

D. All of the above

291. **How did Queen Victoria's husband, Prince Albert, die?**

A. He was assassinated

B. Natural causes

C. In an accident

D. From an illness

292. **When was the Act of Union with Ireland established?**

A. January 1, 1801

B. March 1, 1800

C. December 25, 1802

D. None of the above

293. **What significant social reform occurred during the Victorian era?**

A. Legalization of abortion

B. Abolition of slavery

C. Women's suffrage

D. Prohibition of alcohol

294. **How did Queen Victoria react to her husband's death?**

A. It did not have an effect on her

B. She refused to leave the castle

C. She wore black for the rest of her life

D. She abdicated

295. **What was the main religion in England during this period?**

A. Presbyterianism

B. Buddhism

C. Roman Catholicism

D. Anglicanism

296. **When was the East India Company dissolved?**

A. 1850

B. 1857

C. 1869

D. 1874

297. **How can Britain's foreign policy direction during the Victorian era be best summarized?**

A. It remained largely the same

B. It became more aggressive

C. It was focused on the containment of the United States

D. It was the biggest failure of the Victorian era

298. **When was Lord William Salisbury first elected to the office of prime minister?**

A. 1880

B. 1885

C. 1887

D. 1895

299. **Which royal house did Queen Victoria belong to?**

A. Stuart

B. Windsor

C. Hanover

D. Habsburg

300. To whom was Queen Victoria's eldest daughter, Victoria, married?

    A. Kaiser Frederick II

    B. Kaiser Wilhelm II

    C. Tsar Nicholas

    D. None of the above

301. When did Queen Victoria celebrate her Golden Jubilee?

    A. 1887

    B. 1877

    C. 1867

    D. 1897

302. What did the "Diamond Jubilee" mark?

    A. Half a century of Victoria's rule

    B. Sixty years of Victoria's rule

    C. Celebration of the Glorious Revolution

    D. None of the above

303. Who was the grandfather of Queen Victoria?

    A. George III

    B. Prince Edward

    C. Charles II

    D. James VII and II

304. Who succeeded Queen Victoria as king of the United Kingdom?

    A. George IV

    B. Charles III

    C. Edward VII

    D. James VIII

305. How was Queen Victoria referred to, during her lifetime and afterward, because of her successful and international reign?

    A. The Iron Lady

    B. The Supreme Queen

    C. The Grandmother of Europe

    D. The Arbiter of Europe

Answers

286. A. A constitutional monarchy
287. A. 1851
288. C. Trains
289. B. 1873
290. D. All of the above
291. D. From an illness
292. A. January 1, 1801
293. B. Abolition of slavery
294. C. She wore black for the rest of her life
295. D. Anglicanism
296. D. 1874
297. B. It became more aggressive
298. B. 1885
299. C. Hanover
300. A. Kaiser Frederick II
301. A. 1887
302. B. sixty years of Victoria's rule
303. A. George III
304. C. Edward VII
305. C. The Grandmother of Europe

The Boer Wars and England in South Africa (1899–1902)

The United Kingdom waged two wars against the local Boer population of South Africa during the reign of Queen Victoria. It was a long and difficult conflict that lasted for many years. The British troops faced fierce resistance from the Boer forces in battles fought across the country. As more soldiers were sent from England, new strategies were introduced to try to win the war, but victory was not easy!

306. Who was fighting in the Boer War?

A. France and Germany

B. England and South Africa

C. England and Scotland

D. United States and Mexico

307. Why was there a war between Britain and South Africa?

A. For freedom of religion

B. To gain control over mineral resources

C. To spread European culture

D. Over conflicting political beliefs

308. When did the First Boer War begin?

A. 1878

B. 1880

C. 1882

D. 1884

309. **Which British politician was responsible for annexing South African territories for the British in 1877?**

A. Winston Churchill

B. Lord Salisbury

C. Sir Theophilus Shepstone

D. Robert Baden-Powell

310. **Who declared a state of rebellion in 1899, leading to the Boer War?**

A. Cecil Rhodes

B. Queen Victoria

C. Paul Kruger

D. Robert Baden-Powell

311. **What type of government ruled South Africa at the time of the Boer War?**

A. Republic

B. Monarchy

C. Dictatorship

D. Democracy

312. **Who were known as "Boers" in South Africa during the Boer War?**

A. African tribesmen

B. British settlers

C. Dutch colonists

D. French refugees

313. **What was agreed upon in the peace agreement after the First Boer War?**

A. British rights to South African minerals

B. Different degrees of citizenship for Boers and British

C. Dissolution of the South African Republic

D. Self-governance for the Boers under British protection

314. When did the Second Boer War break out?

   A. 1889

   B. 1890

   C. 1899

   D. 1900

315. How many military casualties did the British suffer during the Boer War?

   A. 90,000

   B. 150,000

   C. 250,000

   D. 350,000

316. Approximately how many civilians were affected by the Second Boer War?

   A. 50,000

   B. 90,000

   C. 130,000

   D. 170,000

317. What does the word "Boer" mean?

   A. Inhabitant

   B. Traveler

   C. Colonist

   D. Farmer

318. Who became one of the leaders of the British Army in early 1900 and swung the tide for the British?

   A. Winston Churchill

   B. Robert Baden-Powell

   C. Lord Kitchener

   D. Douglas Haig

319. Which treaty ended the Second Boer War?

   A. Treaty of Amsterdam

   B. Treaty of Cape Town

   C. Treaty of Williamsburg

   D. Treaty of Vereeniging

320. What was the result of the Boer Wars?

A. British victory

B. South African independence

C. Stalemate

D. None of the above

Answers

306. B. England and South Africa

307. B. To gain control over mineral resources

308. B. 1880

309. C. Sir Theophilus Shepstone

310. C. Paul Kruger

311. A. Republic

312. C. Dutch colonists

313. D. Self-governance of the Boers under British protection

314. C. 1899

315. A. 90,000

316. A. 50,000

317. D. Farmer

318. C. Lord Kitchener

319. D. Treaty of Vereeniging

320. A. British victory

The Edwardian Era (1901–1914)

The Edwardian era was a time of significant change in England from 1901 to 1914. During this period, King Edward VII ruled the country and made many improvements. He brought new technology and ideas that revolutionized transportation, communication, entertainment, fashion—you name it! People had more freedom to travel around the world than ever before. There were exciting new inventions, like cars and airplanes, that changed how people got around. Life during this era was fast-paced and full of fun.

321. **What major advancement in the field of transport coincided with the Edwardian era?**

    A. Invention of railways

    B. Invention of commercial aircrafts

    C. Invention of automobiles

    D. All of the above

322. **When did Edward VII ascend the throne?**

    A. 1901

    B. 1911

    C. 1902

    D. 1903

323. Whose son was Edward VII?

A. Edward VI's

B. Charles III's

C. Queen Victoria's

D. George V's

324. Who founded The National Trust during this period?

A. Charles Darwin

B. Winston Churchill

C. John Ruskin

D. Alfred Nobel

325. How old was Edward VII when he became king?

A. 38

B. 49

C. 54

D. 60

326. Under Edward VII, major reforms were passed in which areas of British life?

A. Industry

B. Social welfare

C. Military

D. Working conditions

327. Which power was the main rival of Great Britain during this time?

A. France

B. Russia

C. Germany

D. None of the above

328. Why are the years 1909-1910 considered the most challenging years of Edward VII's life?

A. Because of the death of his second-born son

B. Because of the ongoing constitutional crisis

C. Because of the outbreak of World War I

D. Because of the economic problems created overseas

329. **Who was the prime minister of Great Britain from 1902 to 1905?**

A. Archibald Primrose

B. J.M Barrie

C. Arthur Balfour

D. H. H. Asquith

330. **Which political party pushed for impressive reforms during the Edwardian era?**

A. The Liberal Party

B. The Conservative Party

C. The Whigs

D. None of the above

331. **When was the Labour Party founded?**

A. 1848

B. 1900

C. 1910

D. None of the above

332. **When did Edward VII die?**

A. 1909

B. 1910

C. 1911

D. 1912

333. **How did industry expand during this time?**

A. Steel production increased

B. New technologies changed working conditions

C. Factories opened around Europe

D. All of the above

334. **Who succeeded Edward VII as king?**

A. Edward VIII

B. George V

C. Charles III

D. Henry IX

335. Which of these statements best describes the domestic situation in Great Britain during the Edwardian era?

A. Great Britain was able to cement its power as a global hegemon

B. Domestic politics were relatively stable and progress-oriented

C. Britain's prime ministers proceeded to break with the will of the monarchy

D. None of the above

Answers

321. C. Invention of automobiles

322. A. 1901

323. C. Queen Victoria's

324. C. John Ruskin

325. D. 60

326. C. Military

327. C. Germany

328. B. Because of the ongoing constitutional crisis

329. C. Arthur Balfour

330. A. The Liberal Party

331. B. 1900

332. B. 1910

333. D. All of the above

334. B. George V

335. B. Domestic politics were relatively stable and progress-oriented

World War I in English History (1914–1918)

World War I was a notable event in English history, beginning in 1914 and ending in 1918. Young men from England were sent to fight in battles across Europe as they sought to protect their homeland. As the war raged on, those at home faced shortages of food and fuel while dealing with the fear of losing loved ones overseas. The brave individuals who fought for their country helped shape our lives today, making World War I an unforgettable part of English history.

336. Who was the leader of England during World War I?

A. King George V

B. Queen Victoria

C. Prime Minister David Lloyd George

D. Winston Churchill

337. Why did England formally enter WWI?

A. To increase its power and land holdings

B. To help Germany win the war

C. To protect Belgium from German invasion

D. To prevent further spread of Communism

338. **How long did World War I last in Europe?**

  A. Two years

  B. Four years

  C. Six months

  D. Ten years

339. **What was the main cause of WWI?**

  A. Unification of Europe

  B. Industrial Revolution

  C. Militarism and alliances

  D. Spread of Communism

340. **Which nations constituted the Entente in WWI, outside of Britain?**

  A. Germany, Austria-Hungary, and Turkey

  B. France, Russia, and the United States

  C. France and Italy

  D. Serbia, Bulgaria, and Japan

341. **Who were known as the "Lost Generation"?**

  A. Soldiers who survived World War I

  B. Civilians who fought in World War I

  C. Artists, writers, and intellectuals affected by WWI

  D. Women involved in war efforts

342. **Who was the British prime minister at the time of the outbreak of the war?**

  A. Winston Churchill

  B. H. H. Asquith

  C. David Lloyd George

  D. Arthur Balfour

343. **In which of these battles did Britain achieve decisive victories?**

  A. Battle of the Somme

  B. Battle of Verdun

  C. First Battle of Ypres

  D. None of the above

344. The leader of which major European superpower that took part in the war was a first cousin of **Britain's** George V?

A. France

B. Austria

C. Russia

D. Prussia

345. When was the Defense of the Realm Act (DORA) passed, giving government an **increased** range of competences during the war?

A. 1914

B. 1915

C. 1916

D. 1917

Answers

336. A. King George V

337. C. To protect Belgium from German invasion

338. B. Four years

339. C. Militarism and alliances

340. B. France, Russia, and the United States

341. C. Artists, writers, and intellectuals affected by WWI

342. B. H. H. Asquith

343. D. None of the above

344. C. Russia

345. A. 1914

Interwar Britain (1918–1939)

Between 1918 and 1939, Great Britain experienced a period of transformation. After World War I ended in 1918, people were eager to put the horrors of war behind them and move on with their lives. Technological advances brought new industries, and improved transportation systems connected cities throughout the country like never before. Although there were hardships during this time known as interwar Britain, it was also a period filled with creativity, progress, and optimism for what could come next!

346. What was the name of the British prime minister from 1937 to 1940?

A. Neville Chamberlain

B. Winston Churchill

C. Stanley Baldwin

D. Clement Attlee

347. In what year did women first get the right to vote in Britain?

A. 1918

B. 1928

C. 1938

D. 1935

348. How many countries were part of the League of Nations when it formed in 1920?

A. 10

B. 23

C. 20

D. 42

349. Which European power was forced to pay massive war reparations according to the Treaty of Versailles?

A. Germany

B. France

C. Italy

D. Austria

350. What was the principal declared objective of the League of Nations?

A. To contain the rise of Germany

B. To stop the spread of Communism

C. To maintain world peace

D. All of the above

351. What was the name of the British Empire's first battle cruiser, built in 1907?

A. HMS *Dreadnaught*

B. HMS *Eagle*

C. HMS *Argus*

D. HMS *Invincible*

352. Which political party gained power in 1924 after winning a landslide victory?

A. Labour Party

B. Conservative Party

C. Liberal Party

D. Communist Party

353. In what year did Britain and Ireland sign the Anglo-Irish Treaty, effectively forming the Irish Free State?

A. 1919

B. 1921

C. 1928

D. 1931

354. Who was the first woman elected to Parliament in Britain?

A. Nancy Astor

B. Emmeline Pankhurst

C. Margaret Thatcher

D. Tiffany Brooks

355. What event caused economic depression and high unemployment rates throughout 1930s Britain?

A. The Wall Street Crash

B. Formation of the Soviet Union

C. Prohibition

D. Industrial Revolution

356. Where were the peace talks held between the participants of WWI?

A. Berlin

B. London

C. Washington

D. Paris

357. About how many British soldiers died in WWI?

A. 3,000,000

B. 6,000,000

C. 800,000

D. 1,300,000

358. Who wrote *The Road to Wigan Pier*, a book about working class life in interwar Britain?

A. J.R.R. Tolkien

B. George Orwell

C. Virginia Woolf

D. H.G. Wells

359. In what year did unemployment peak under Prime Minister Ramsay MacDonald's government?

A. 1929

B. 1932

C. 1935

D. 1938

360. Which party formed the government in Britain in 1924?

A. Conservatives

B. Labour

C. Liberals

D. Whigs

361. Which new state did Britain recognize in early February of 1924?

A. Empire of Japan

B. German Federal Republic

C. Soviet Union

D. Yugoslavia

362. In what year was the Citizens Advice Bureau founded by a group of charities, lawyers, and social reformers?

A. 1939

B. 1925

C. 1929

D. 1935

363. The rule of which British monarch was subject to a constitutional crisis in 1936?

A. George V

B. Edward VII

C. George VI

D. Edward VIII

364. When did the British government launch a national rearmament program, following similar efforts from Nazi Germany?

A. 1933

B. 1934

C. 1935

D. 1936

365. In what year did King George V make his first royal Christmas broadcast to the British people?

A. 1925

B. 1932

C. 1935

D. 1940

Answers

346. A. Neville Chamberlain

347. A. 1918

348. D. 42

349. A. Germany

350. C. To maintain world peace

351. D. HMS *Invincible*

352. B. Conservative Party

353. B. 1921

354. A. Nancy Astor

355. A. The Wall Street Crash

356. D. Paris

357. C. 800,000

358. B. George Orwell

359. C. 1935

360. B. Labour

361. C. Soviet Union

362. A. 1939

363. D. Edward VIII

364. B. 1934

365. B. 1932

The General Strike in England (1926)

In 1926, England experienced a big event called the General Strike. It was when millions of workers went on strike to protest unfair working conditions and wages. For nine days, large parts of the country stopped running as people all over showed their support for the cause. This historic moment changed Britain forever!

366. How long did the General Strike of 1926 last?

A. Two days

B. Ten weeks

C. Four months

D. Nine days

367. Who called for the General Strike?

A. The British Army

B. Trade unions

C. The Labour Party

D. Prime minister

368. Why was the strike held?

A. To protest reduced wages

B. To end the rule of the Conservative government

C. To promote democracy

D. None of the above

369. Which group of workers were concerned the most with the strike?

A. Doctors and nurses

B. Steel workers

C. Lawyers

D. Coal miners

370. What was the result of the General Strike?

A. The government was changed

B. The strike was called off after a stalemate

C. Employers gave higher wages to their workforce

D. None of the above

371. What was the average wage for miners by the time of the strike?

A. Three pounds

B. Six pounds

C. Eight pounds

D. Nine pounds

372. When did the strike begin?

A. May 1

B. May 4

C. May 10

D. May 15

373. About how many people participated in the strike?

A. Ten million

B. Two million

C. Five million

D. Eight hundred thousand

374. Which of these statements is true about the economic situation of post-WWI Britain?

A. Britain was the richest nation on earth

B. Britain had a relatively stable economy

C. Britain suffered the most from the 1929 Great Depression

D. None of the above

375. Which of these was not among the demands of the workers during the 1926 General Strike?

A. Increasing the cost of living

B. Increasing the wages

C. Decreasing working hours

D. Granting more rights to trade unions

Answers

366. D. Nine days
367. B. Trade unions
368. A. To protest reduced wages
369. D. Coal miners
370. B. The strike was called off after a stalemate
371. A. Three pounds
372. B. May 4
373. B. Two million
374. B. Britain had a relatively stable economy
375. A. Increasing the cost of living

The Great Depression in England (1929–1939)

The Great Depression was a difficult time for England between 1929 and 1939. Many people struggled to put food on the table, others couldn't find jobs, and some even lost their homes. It was an incredibly tough period in history that made life hard for families nationwide. People had to get creative and work together to survive these trying times.

376. What event began the Great Depression in England?

A. The Wall Street Crash of 1929

B. World War I

C. The rise of Nazi Germany

D. The influenza pandemic

377. Which English prime minister helped introduce social welfare during the Great Depression?

A. Winston Churchill

B. David Lloyd George

C. Neville Chamberlain

D. Clement Attlee

378. Which statement is true about unemployment levels in Britain during this period?

A. They remained mostly steady

B. They increased by a noticeable amount

C. They drastically decreased

D. None of the above

379. Which of these areas was hit the hardest with economic problems caused by the Great Depression?

A. London

B. Dover

C. Birmingham

D. None of the above

380. How did disruptions in trade affect England's economy during the Great Depression?

A. It created more competition from other countries

B. It encouraged global economic growth

C. It resulted in lower prices and increased exports

D. It contributed to the rise of unemployment

381. Why do historians consider the destructive results of the Great Depression in Britain relatively modest?

A. Because of the staunch policies of the government

B. Because of the charities set up by the monarchy

C. Because of the already strong economy it had

D. Because of the recession it had already been experiencing before 1929

382. When did the British government switch back to the gold standard after WWI?

A. 1921

B. 1925

C. 1929

D. 1933

383. When did Britain begin to recover from the Great Depression?

    A. 1930

    B. 1933

    C. 1939

    D. 1940

384. What was only way people were able to cope economically with the effects of the Great Depression?

    A. By gambling

    B. By relying on charitable donations

    C. By spending less and saving more

    D. None of the above

385. How did the Great Depression in England end?

    A. With a new economic stimulus plan

    B. With the introduction of rationing

    C. With military victory against Germany

    D. With an increase in global trade

Answers

376. A. The Wall Street Crash of 1929

377. B. David Lloyd George

378. B. They increased by a noticeable amount

379. C. Birmingham

380. D. It contributed to the rise of unemployment

381. D. Because of the recession it had been experiencing before 1929

382. B. 1925

383. B. 1933

384. C. By spending less and saving more

385. C. With military victory against Germany

England's Involvement in World War II (1939–1945)

When World War II broke out in 1939, England was one of the first countries to join the fight. For six long years, brave British people worked together to protect their country and stand up for freedom globally. They faced many challenges along the way as they fought against Nazi forces. But despite all odds, England persevered and helped bring about a victorious end to WWII!

386. Who was England's leader during WWII?

    A. Winston Churchill

    B. Queen Elizabeth II

    C. Adolf Hitler

    D. Franklin Roosevelt

387. When did Germany invade Poland, causing Britain to declare war on them?

    A. June 8, 1938

    B. September 1, 1939

    C. December 5, 1941

    D. April 15, 1945

388. In what year did Japan attack Pearl Harbor, bringing America into the war as an ally of Britain and other Allied countries?

A. May 9, 1941

B. December 8, 1941

C. June 22, 1942

D. April 28, 1945

389. On which war theater were British forces most concentrated throughout the war?

A. The Pacific Theater

B. The Eastern Front

C. The Western Front

D. The North African Theater

390. Who were Britain's main allies during World War II?

A. Germany, Japan, and Italy

B. France, the US, and the USSR

C. France, Germany, and Spain

D. None of the above

Answers

386. A. Winston Churchill

387. B. September 1,1939

388. B. December 8,1941

389. C. The Western Front

390. B. France, the US, and the USSR

The Blitz (1940–1941)

years, the British people demonstrated extraordinary courage and resilience, especially during the Blitz—a relentless bombing campaign by German forces from 1940 to 1941. Cities were shattered, lives disrupted, yet the spirit of unity and defiance never wavered. Against overwhelming odds, Britain stood firm, playing a vital role in the Allied victory and the global fight for freedom.

391. What was the goal of the Blitz?

A. To conquer England

B. To destroy military targets

C. To demoralize civilians

D. All of the above

392. Why were people evacuated from their homes during the Blitz?

A. To keep them safe from bombings

B. To make room for German soldiers

C. To provide them with better living conditions

D. To find work in other cities

393. From which word does the word "Blitz" originate?

A. Blitzcrank

B. Blitzkrieg

C. Blitzortung

D. None of the above

394. **How did the British people respond to the Blitz?**

    A. They surrendered to German forces

    B. They fled their homes

    C. They fought back with military force

    D. They stayed in their homes and endured

395. **When did the bombing of London begin?**

    A. September 1, 1940

    B. September 7, 1940

    C. September 21, 1940

    D. September 26, 1940

396. **When did the Battle of Britain begin?**

    A. July 1940

    B. February 1941

    C. October 1940

    D. December 1940

397. **Who oversaw planning the attacks on Britain during the Blitz?**

    A. Adolf Hitler

    B. Joseph Goebbels

    C. Joseph Stalin

    D. Hermann Goering

398. **What was used as an effective bomb shelter against the Germans by the population of London?**

    A. Tower Bridge

    B. London Underground

    C. Westminster Abbey

    D. All of the above

399. **Who won the Battle of Britain?**

    A. Great Britain

    B. Nazi Germany

    C. Soviet Union

    D. It was a draw

400. How many British casualties were caused by the Blitz?

    A. 10,000–20,000

    B. 50,000–60,000

    C. 100,000–150,000

    D. 200,000–300,000

Answers

391. D. All of the above
392. A. To keep them safe from bombings
393. B. Blitzkrieg
394. D. They stayed in their homes and endured
395. B. September 7, 1940
396. A. July 1940
397. D. Hermann Goering
398. B. London Underground
399. A. Great Britain
400. C. 100,000–150,000

The Cold War in Relation to England (1947–1991)

England was part of the Cold War from 1947 to 1991. This war was between two competing superpowers, the United States and Russia. It was a time of tension, distrust, and fear as both sides built up weapons to gain power over each other. England played a significant role during this period as it provided support for one side against the other. The Cold War had a notable impact on people's lives all around the world!

401. What was the purpose of the talks held by the victorious nations in WWII?

    A. To stop Communism from spreading

    B. To protect democratic governments

    C. To create a new world order

    D. All of the above

402. How did Britain respond to Soviet aggression during the Cold War?

    A. With military action

    B. By allying with the United States

    C. By strengthening its economy

    D. It didn't respond

403. After WWII, what was the main measure Britain resorted to for protection from a potential Soviet threat during the Cold War?

A. It formed a nuclear arsenal

B. It developed stronger ties with France

C. It increased trade restrictions on Russia

D. It decreased social spending

404. During which of the following events did the Cold War reach its peak?

A. The Cuban Missile Crisis

B. The collapse of the Soviet Union

C. The fall of Communism

D. The rise of nuclear weapons

405. How did Britain react to the dissolution of the Soviet Union in 1991?

A. It took part in efforts to build up Russia

B. It increased military expenditure

C. It withdrew from NATO

D. It reduced its international presence

406. What was one outcome of Britain's involvement in the Cold War?

A. An increase in global trade

B. An end to poverty across Europe

C. Heightened tensions between East and West

D. Improved relations with former enemies

407. Why is Winston's Churchill's speech in March 1946 considered important in this context?

A. It is considered the exact beginning of the Cold War

B. It presented the US and the UK as the defenders of a new world order

C. It heavily criticized the actions of the US government during WWII

D. It wished for a dissolution of the Soviet Union

408. What was one major consequence of increased tensions between East and West during the Cold War?

A. The development of new weapons technologies

B. Increased global trade

C. Increased economic prosperity in Europe

D. The rise of global Communism

409. What metaphor did Winston Churchill use to describe the political and ideological isolation of the USSR and the Communist states from the rest of the world in his 1946 speech?

A. Iron Man

B. Iron Wall

C. Iron Curtain

D. Iron Window

410. When did the Berlin Wall come down?

A. 1941

B. 1947

C. 1989

D. 1991

411. Which German territory did the British control after the Allied occupation following WWII?

A. Northeast

B. Northwest

C. Southeast

D. Southwest

412. How did Britain's involvement in the Cold War ultimately affect Europe?

A. It led to stronger military capabilities in the West

B. It improved economic prosperity across Europe

C. It caused an arms race among nations

D. All of the above

413. What was one consequence of the Cuban Missile Crisis?

A. Increased military spending by Britain

B. The dissolution of NATO

C. Improved relations with former Communist states

D. Heightened tensions between the USSR and the US

414. Which of the following is true about the military involvement of Britain during the conflicts of the Cold War?

A. Britain was never involved in military conflicts during the Cold War

B. Britain's involvement in military conflicts during the Cold War was minimal

C. Britain was actively involved in military conflicts during the Cold War

D. Britain exclusively pledged economic support for military conflicts during the Cold War

415. What was the result of the elections held in the UK after WWII?

A. Conservative victory

B. Liberal Party was victorious

C. Labour Party gained power

D. None of the above

416. What was a major consequence for the British Empire after WWII?

A. Britain was forced to give up all claims to its colonial territories immediately

B. Britain has kept its overseas territories after WWII

C. Britain had to gradually decolonize

D. None of the above

417. What was "The Troubles"?

A. An ethno-nationalist conflict in Ireland

B. A period of austerity under the Labour government

C. A three-year economic crisis

D. None of the above

418. When did the UK become part of the European Union?

A. 1970

B. 1973

C. 1975

D. 1977

419. How did the Cold War end?

A. With the signing of the Treaty of Paris

B. With military action from both sides

C. With an agreement between East and West Germany

D. With the dissolution of Soviet Union

420. Which decade can be considered the most prosperous in Britain after WWII?

A. 1990s

B. 1980s

C. 1970s

D. 1950s

Answers

401. D. All of the above

402. B. By allying with the United States

403. A. It formed a nuclear arsenal

404. A. The Cuban Missile Crisis

405. A. It took part in efforts to build up Russia

406. D. Improved relations with former enemies

407. B. It presented the US and the UK as the defenders of a new world order

408. A. The development of new weapons technologies

409. C. Iron Curtain

410. C. 1989

411. B. Northwest

412. D. All of the above

413. D. Heightened tensions between the USSR and the US

414. C. Britain was actively involved in military conflicts during the Cold War

415. C. Labour Party gained power

416. C. Britain had to gradually decolonize

417. A. An ethno-nationalist conflict in Ireland

418. B. 1973

419. D. With the dissolution of Soviet Union

420. D. 1950s

The Coronation of Queen Elizabeth II (1953)

On the June 2, 1953, Queen Elizabeth II was formally crowned. She had been queen since February 6 of that same year when her father, King George VI, died. Thousands of people globally gathered to watch the coronation and celebrate Queen Elizabeth's reign as Britain's new monarch. It was a magnificent event with music, pageantry, and grandeur rarely seen in history!

421. When did the coronation ceremony of Queen Elizabeth II take place?

    A. December 25, 1950

    B. June 2,1953

    C. May 14, 1952

    D. September 21,1955

422. What is known as "the traditional crown" of the British monarchy?

    A. The Crown Jewels

    B. The Imperial State Crown

    C. St. Edward's Crown

    D. Royal Sceptre

423. Where did Queen Elizabeth take her coronation oath?

A. Westminster Abbey

B. Buckingham Palace

C. Windsor Castle

D. Tower of London

424. How old was Queen Elizabeth when she took the throne in 1952?

A. 21 years old

B. 25 years old

C. 26 years old

D. 18 years old

425. Who designed Queen Elizabeth II's coronation gown?

A. Norman Hartnell

B. Michael Kors

C. Vivienne Westwood

D. Hans Wegner

Answers

421. B. June 2, 1953
422. C. St. Edward's Crown
423. A. Westminster Abbey
424. B. 25 years old
425. A. Norman Hartnell

Margaret Thatcher Era (1979–1990)

Margaret Thatcher was Britain's first female prime minister and served from 1979 to 1990. During her time in office, she earned the nickname "The Iron Lady" for her ambitious and determined leadership style. Her policies included privatizing government services and industries and reducing income inequality through a series of social reforms. She also worked to strengthen Britain's foreign policy by negotiating with notable allies globally. This period in British history is known as the Margaret Thatcher era—an era filled with bold decision-making that shaped modern Britain!

426. What did Mrs. Thatcher do to help revive Britain's economy in the 1980s?

A. Introduced free healthcare for all citizens

B. Lowered taxes across the country

C. Nationalized many industries

D. Increased government spending

427. What international event happened early in Mrs. Thatcher's time as prime minister?

A. Communism fell in Eastern Europe

B. The Falklands War

C. Brexiteer movement began

D. NATO was expelled from Western Europe

428. What nickname was given to Mrs. Thatcher's economic policies by her opponents?

A. Iron Lady

B. The Great Communicator

C. TINA (there is no alternative)

D. Thatcherism

429. What did Margaret Thatcher do to try to reduce the influence of trade unions?

A. Introduced strict laws to limit their power

B. Raised taxes on union members

C. Encouraged workers' rights

D. Nationalized all corporations

430. What was Mrs. Thatcher famous for saying about freedom and capitalism?

A. Socialism works best when given a chance

B. Freedom means taking control of your own destiny

C. Capitalism must be regulated by governments

D. There is no such thing as free markets

431. How did Mrs. Thatcher's economic policies effect industry in Britain during the 1980s?

A. She closed down many factories

B. Increased government spending on new businesses

C. Tax cuts made it more profitable to invest in industry

D. She nationalized all corporations

432. By what nickname is Margaret Thatcher known today?

A. The Iron Lady

B. The Communicator

C. The Arbiter of Europe

D. The Labour Nightmare

433. What did Margaret Thatcher do with regard to taxes during the 1980s?

A. Raised them for everyone

B. Lowered them for the higher classes

C. Introduced a flat rate tax system

D. Abolished income taxes altogether

434. How did Mrs. Thatcher's economic policies impact Britain's manufacturing sector?

A. They caused it to collapse completely

B. The sector was nationalized

C. It saw rapid growth as taxes were cut

D. She implemented strict regulations in the industry

435. What did Margaret Thatcher do to promote home ownership?

A. Nationalized all housing

B. Introduced the Right to Buy legislation

C. Encouraged private landlords

D. Lowered interest rates on mortgages

436. How did Mrs. Thatcher's economic policies impact unemployment levels during her time in office?

A. They increased significantly

B. They stayed the same

C. Tax cuts made it easier to find jobs

D. They were reduced

437. Which organization attempted to assassinate Margaret Thatcher in October of 1984?

A. ISIS

B. IRA

C. The Black Hands

D. The International

438. How were Mrs. Thatcher's economic policies received by the Labour Party?

    A. They were welcomed

    B. Criticized for being too extreme

    C. Seen as an improvement compared to previous governments

    D. Ignored completely

439. In which European city did Margaret Thatcher give a speech in which she opposed the idea of a federal Europe?

    A. Bruges

    B. Brussels

    C. Paris

    D. Madrid

440. Until when was Margaret Thatcher the prime minister?

    A. 1989

    B. 1990

    C. 1991

    D. 1992

Answers

426. B. Lowered taxes across the country

427. B. The Falklands War

428. D. Thatcherism

429. A. Introduced strict laws to limit their power

430. B. Freedom means taking control of your own destiny

431. C. Tax cuts made it more profitable to invest in industry

432. A. The Iron Lady

433. B. Lowered them for the higher classes

434. C. It saw rapid growth as taxes were cut

435. B. Introduced the Right to Buy legislation

436. D. They were reduced

437. B. IRA

438. B. Criticized for being too extreme

439. A. Bruges

440. B. 1990

The Miners' Strike (1984–1985)

The Miners' Strike of 1984 was the longest strike in British history. Miners from all over Britain went on a massive strike for one year, starting in 1984 and ending in 1985. They were fighting against their employers' plans to close some of their coal mines. It was cold outside, but the miners stayed determined to make sure their voices would be heard! Despite many hardships, it was an inspiring event that had repercussions across the country and around the world.

441. What triggered the Miners' Strike of 1984?

    A. The introduction of new technology by the mining companies

    B. A dispute over pay and job security

    C. The closure of several coal mines in Scotland

    D. An increase in fuel prices for miners

442. How long did the strike last?

    A. one week

    B. two months

    C. six months

    D. eleven months

443. Who was prime minister during this time?

    A. John Major

    B. Margaret Thatcher

    C. Tony Blair

    D. Gordon Brown

444. Who led the miners during this period?

A. Arthur Scargill

B. David Cameron

C. Harold Wilson

D. Ian MacGregor

445. How did the workers primarily protest?

A. Using armed violence

B. Mass demonstrations

C. Non-violent civil disobedience

D. None of the above

446. What were some of the consequences of the strike for communities?

A. Job losses

B. Increased unemployment

C. Closures in local businesses

D. All of the above

447. What did mining companies accuse Arthur Scargill and his union of doing during this period?

A. Prolonging violence

B. Destroying morale

C. Encouraging a militant approach

D. None of the above

448. What was the outcome of the strike?

A. It was ruled illegal

B. A pay raise and job security

C. A complete firing of the miners

D. Privatization of the coal industry in 1985

449. Where did one of the most violent clashes between police and protesters take place in June 1984?

A. Birmingham

B. London

C. Yorkshire

D. Orgreave

450. How much money was given to striking miners by the National Union of Mineworkers (NUM)?

A. £2 million

B. £5 million

C. £8 million

D. £10 million

Answers

441. B. A dispute over pay and job security
442. D. eleven months
443. B. Margaret Thatcher
444. A. Arthur Scargill
445. C. Non-violent civil disobedience
446. D. All of the above
447. C. Encouraging a militant approach
448. A. It was ruled illegal
449. D. Orgreave
450. C. £8 Million

The Good Friday Agreement (1998)

The Good Friday Agreement was signed by many people who wanted a better future for the country. This agreement helped end years of violence between different groups and allowed everyone to live side-by-side in peace. Everyone promised to respect each other's cultures, traditions, and beliefs so that all people could live free from fear or discrimination. With this new agreement came the hope that things would get better!

451. What is the Good Friday Agreement?

   A. A peace agreement signed in 1998 to end conflict between Ireland and Northern Ireland

   B. A law passed by British Parliament in 1989 outlawing discrimination against minorities

   C. An international treaty that ended a long-standing border dispute between two countries

   D. The document outlining the terms for Scotland's independence from England

452. Who were involved with signing the Good Friday Agreement?

A. Representatives of the Irish Republican Army (IRA), loyalist paramilitary organizations, and representatives from Britain, Europe, and the US State Department

B. Only representatives from Britain

C. Only representatives from the Irish Republic

D. The prime ministers of UK/Ireland

453. What were the main outcomes of the Good Friday Agreement?

A. The end of sectarian violence in Northern Ireland

B. The establishment of a government in which nationalists and unionists shared power

C. The secession of Northern Island from the United Kingdom

D. Recognition of Scotland's independence

454. Where was the Good Friday Agreement signed?

A. London, England

B. Belfast, Northern Ireland

C. Dublin, Republic of Ireland

D. Washington, D.C.

455. What is the legal name of the Good Friday Agreement?

A. The Republic of Ireland Peace Treaty

B. The Belfast Agreement

C. The British Irish Intergovernmental Conference

D. The Anglo-Irish Agreement

456. Who was a major negotiator for the Good Friday Agreement, earning him a Nobel Peace Prize?

A. Former Prime Minister Tony Blair

B. Former US President Bill Clinton

C. Former First Minister of Northern Ireland David Trimble

D. Sinn Féin leader Gerry Adams

457. When was the agreement signed?

A. May 22, 1998

B. April 25, 1998

C. April 10, 1998

D. May 19, 1998

458. What did British Prime Minister Tony Blair say about the Good Friday Agreement?

A. It was an important step toward peace in Northern Ireland

B. It was a mistake to sign the agreement

C. The agreement would have no impact on life in Northern Ireland

D. None of the above

459. What does the Good Friday Agreement guarantee?

A. Protection of minority rights in Northern Ireland and Ireland

B. Equal voting rights among the Irish and the Northern Irish

C. Freedom of religion

D. None of the above

460. How has the Good Friday Agreement affected politics in Northern Ireland since 1998?

A. It has resulted in more violence between Catholics and Protestants

B. It has helped create stability between unionists and nationalists

C. It has led to increased tensions between the two sides

D. It has had no impact on politics in Northern Ireland

Answers

451. A. A peace agreement signed in 1998 to end conflict between Ireland and Northern Ireland

452. A. Representatives of the Irish Republican Army (IRA), loyalist paramilitary organizations, and representatives from Britain, Europe, and the US State Department

453. A. The end of sectarian violence in Northern Ireland

454. B. Belfast, Northern Ireland

455. B. The Belfast Agreement

456. C. Former First Minister of Northern Ireland David Trimble

457. C. April 10, 1998

458. A. It was an important step toward peace in Northern Ireland

459. A. Protection of minority rights in Northern Ireland and Ireland

460. B. It has helped create stability between unionists and nationalists

Modern Britain (2000s–present)

Welcome to modern Britain! In the 2000s, life in Britain has drastically changed. People travel faster and connect globally with new technologies such as smartphones and high-speed internet. Businesses have grown bigger, cities are much more diverse, and people enjoy a variety of cultures. Despite these changes, traditional British values remain, such as politeness, punctuality, and respect for other people's beliefs. Come explore this exciting new era of Britain with us!

461. What is the capital of England?

A. London

B. Manchester

C. Birmingham

D. Liverpool

462. Which is not a member state of the United Kingdom?

A. Wales

B. Northern Ireland

C. Scotland

D. Ireland

463. Who was prime minister from 2007–2010?

A. Gordon Brown

B. Tony Blair

C. David Cameron

D. Theresa May

464. Alongside which two other countries did Britain join the European Union?

    A. Norway and Sweden

    B. Spain and Greece

    C. Ireland and Poland

    D. Denmark and Ireland

465. Who became prime minister of the UK in 2010?

    A. Tony Blair

    B. David Cameron

    C. Liz Truss

    D. Boris Johnson

466. How many members of Parliament are there in Britain?

    A. 500

    B. 650

    C. 750

    D. 900

467. In what year did same-sex marriage become legal in the UK?

    A. 2010

    B. 2013

    C. 2014

    D. 2016

468. What was the national anthem of England until 2022?

    A. "Land of Hope and Glory"

    B. "God Save The Queen"

    C. "Rule Britannia"

    D. "Jerusalem"

469. Who became the prime minister of the UK in October 2022?

    A. Rishi Sunak

    B. David Cameron

    C. Gordon Brown

    D. Tony Blair

470. What type of government does Britain have?

A. Republic

B. Constitutional monarchy

C. Democracy

D. Autocracy

471. When did the Scottish Independence Referendum take place?

A. 2007

B. 2010

C. 2014

D. 2019

472. What is the official religion of England?

A. Anglicanism

B. Catholicism

C. Lutheranism

D. None of the above

473. How many members are there in the House of Lords?

A. 800

B. 950

C. 1100

D. The number changes

474. Who is responsible for making laws in Britain?

A. Prime minister

B. Parliament

C. Queen

D. Citizens

475. Which color does not appear on the British flag?

A. Blue

B. Red

C. White

D. Green

476. In what year did the Conservative Party fail to secure the majority in Parliament, leading to first hung Parliament since 1974?

A. 2001

B. 2010

C. 2014

D. 2005

477. When did the British government hold a referendum to leave the European Union?

A. 2010

B. 2012

C. 2014

D. 2016

478. What is the main currency in Britain?

A. Euro

B. Pound sterling

C. Dollar

D. Mark

479. Who was the prime minister at the time of the Brexit referendum?

A. Theresa May

B. Gordon Brown

C. David Cameron

D. Tony Blair

480. Approximately what percentage of voters voted for Brexit?

A. 48 percent

B. 52 percent

C. 59 percent

D. 61 percent

481. Who became the leader of the Conservative Party in 2019?

A. Theresa May

B. David Cameron

C. Boris Johnson

D. Rishi Sunak

482. What animal appears on British coins and notes?

    A. Lion

    B. Fox

    C. Bull

    D. Eagle

483. When was the Scottish Parliament established?

    A. 1999

    B. 2003

    C. 2005

    D. 2007

484. What is the population of Scotland as of 2019?

    A. four million

    B. five million

    C. eight million

    D. ten million

485. Who was the prime minister during the 2003 invasion of Iraq?

    A. David Cameron

    B. John Major

    C. Gordon Brown

    D. Tony Blair

486. When were the "7/7" bombings carried out in London?

    A. 2001

    B. 2002

    C. 2005

    D. 2007

487. How many members are there in the House of Commons?

    A. 500

    B. 650

    C. 750

    D. 900

488. What color appears on British passport covers?

    A. Blue

    B. Red

    C. White

    D. Green

489. Who is the current prime minister in Scotland?

    A. Nicola Sturgeon

    B. David Cameron

    C. Alex Salmond

    D. John Swinney

490. Who was the most recent female prime minister of Britain?

    A. Margaret Thatcher

    B. Ursula von der Leyen

    C. Liz Truss

    D. None of the above

Answers

461. A. London
462. D. Ireland
463. A. Gordon Brown
464. D. Denmark and Ireland
465. B. David Cameron
466. B. 650
467. B. 2013
468. B. "God Save The Queen"
469. A. Rishi Sunak
470. B. Constitutional monarchy
471. C. 2014
472. A. Anglicanism
473. D. The number changes
474. B. Parliament
475. D. Green
476. B. 2010
477. D. 2016
478. B. Pound sterling
479. C. David Cameron
480. B. 52 percent
481. C. Boris Johnson
482. A. Lion
483. A. 1999
484. B. five million
485. D. Tony Blair
486. C. 2005
487. B. 650
488. A. Blue
489. D. John Swinney
490. C. Liz Truss

Coronation of King Charles III (2023)

Everyone in the kingdom gathered around to witness the coronation of King Charles III. Music filled the air as people cheered and celebrated his becoming king. He made his way through an archway of decorated flags, with a crown atop his head. All eyes were on him as he took his place on the throne under a royal canopy made from velvet and jewels. The celebration marked a new beginning for their beloved country, and all rejoiced at this momentous occasion!

491. Who crowned King Charles III as monarch of the United Kingdom?

A. Prince William

B. Archbishop of Canterbury

C. Queen Elizabeth II

D. Prime Minister Liz Truss

492. What were some elements included in the coronation ceremony for King Charles III?

A. Sword and scepter

B. Blessing from God

C. Oath to protect Britain

D. All of the above

493. How many people attended the coronation ceremony for King Charles III?

A. 1,500

B. More than 2,000

C. 700

D. 1,000

494. Which two members of the royal family stood with King Charles III during the coronation ceremony?

A. Prince William and Queen Elizabeth II

B. Princess Anne and Prince Harry

C. Prince William and Queen Camilla

D. Duke of Edinburgh and Duchess of Cornwall

495. Who wrote the prayer recited at the coronation ceremony for King Charles III?

A. Archbishop Justin Welby

B. Prime Minister Theresa May

C. King George VI

D. Queen Victoria

496. What type of traditional musical performances were performed by the Bands Of His Majesty's Royal Marines?

A. Jazz music

B. Classical or traditional music

C. Rock music

D. Pop music

497. What is a new role given to King Charles III as part ruler of the realm?

A. Head of government

B. Head of state

C. Commander in chief

D. Ambassador for the UK

498. What was the name of King Charles III's coronation anthem?

A. "God Save Our Gracious King"

B. "Rule Britannia"

C. "Crown Him With Many Crowns"

D. "Jerusalem"

499. Who led the recitation at the coronation ceremony for King Charles III?

A. Archbishop Justin Welby

B. Queen Elizabeth II

C. Prince William

D. Prime Minister Theresa May

500. Who gave a speech in honor of King Charles III during his coronation ceremony?

A. Archbishop Justin Welby

B. Queen Elizabeth II

C. Prince William

D. Prime Minister Theresa May

Answers

491. B. Archbishop of Canterbury
492. D. All of the above
493. B. More than 2,000
494. C. Prince William and Queen Camilla
495. A. Archbishop Justin Welby
496. B. Classical or traditional music
497. B. Head of state
498. A. "God Save Our Gracious King"
499. A. Archbishop Justin Welby
500. C. Prince William

Conclusion

The history of England is a long and winding trail full of surprises. From the days when English kings reigned over an island nation to today's diverse cultural landscape, this country has been through many changes. It has had its share of great leaders and notorious villains who have all left their mark on modern-day Britain.

England has seen significant social change throughout its past, from the Industrial Revolution, which brought sweeping technological advancements that transformed life for millions, to more recent events such as Brexit, which will shape British politics for years or even decades to come. No matter how much changes, however, certain constants remain: England's commitment to democracy and human rights and her fierce sense of justice tempered by mercy and compassion toward others less fortunate. These values are what truly define the British people regardless of their ethnic or religious backgrounds or political opinions.

Britain may be small, but it continuously plays a notable role on the world stage. Through its economic power, global influence, and strong cultural heritage, it has earned a unique place in history as one of Europe's most prominent countries. Its future may be uncertain, but England's past is an inspiring legacy to follow—one that will continue to shape lives for generations to come.

Part 2: Notable Figures in English History

Illuminating the Lives and Impact of England's Prominent Icons Across the Centuries

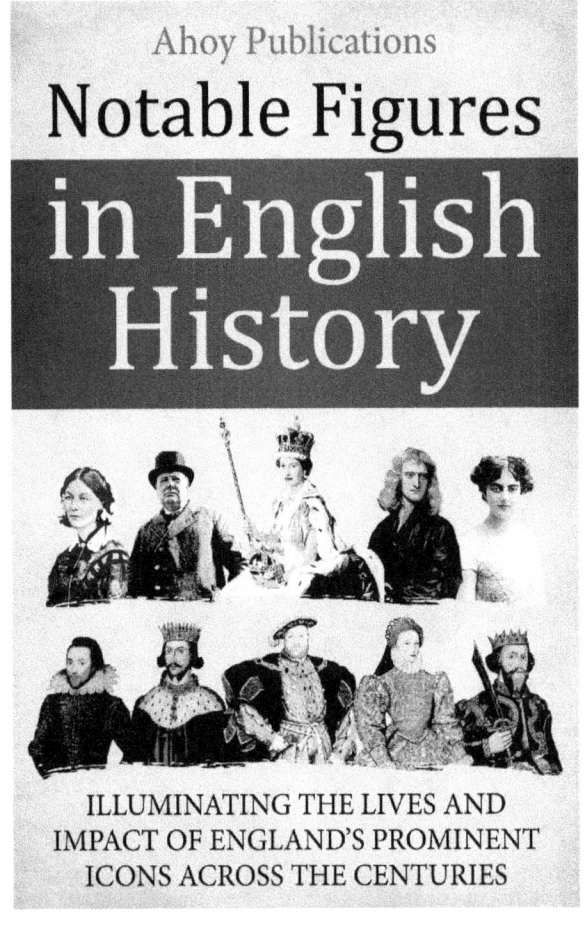

Introduction

If history is a complex narrative of events that are chained together and precipitate each other, it is also a narrative being propelled forward by an endless array of characters and their decisions. Fate sometimes plays its hand as well, but even when that happens, humans are still the ones who determine the course of events through the ways in which they respond to fate. History has witnessed many great men and women who have made choices or pursued goals that have irreversibly altered the chain of events. A considerable portion of these people have been English or in some way associated with England.

The comparatively small English realm and the unified monarchies it has spawned over the centuries have dramatically affected the course of history in many ways relating to science, politics, art, and much more. Such a prominent role on the historical stage inevitably entails certain controversies, but when all is said and done, England has left an enormous mark on the course of mankind, and history would be difficult to imagine without it. That mark has included many monumental events, discoveries, inventions, and innovations, without which the world of today would probably be unrecognizable.

Many characters have played important parts in this tale, and exploring their lives and individual historical epochs is one of the best ways to understand the progression of England's eventful history. The stories of these important historical figures are simultaneously the stories of how a relatively small country, which began as a distant Roman province, became one of the greatest maritime powers and a pioneer of global exploration and conquest. Far from being a simple tale of physical expansion, the history of England is also one of ingenuity, progress, philosophy, and cultural dominance well into modern times.

This book will dive into the lives and legacies of the most notable figures of English history, including medieval rulers, inventors, literary minds, philosophers, wartime leaders, artists, and others. Once these eternal legacies are understood through the human lenses of those who left them behind, it becomes easier to see how England's social, cultural, scientific, and political landscapes have been shaped over centuries of human action. England has been one of the most influential civilizations over the past millennium, and studying its history is also, in many ways, the study of world history.

Focusing specifically on the lives and work of the most notable figures also helps condense what is otherwise a long and complex history into a comprehensive narrative that's easier to digest. The human history of the British Isles extends hundreds of millennia into prehistory, but to grasp the role of England in shaping today's world, it's sufficient to pick up the story in the Middle Ages. This is the era in which most of the great European powers began to evolve into their later form, rising from the chaos that ensued after Western Rome fell. Roman expansion and rule in Britain are often cited as particularly important points in England's early development, but the centuries that followed were the time when England truly embarked on its own unique path.

Chapter 1: William the Conqueror and Henry II: Foundations of a Nation

Like many other parts of the world that are now cut off by water, England was permanently settled by anatomically modern humans during the Last Glacial Period around 11,000 to 13,000 years ago. At that time, lower sea levels allowed for land crossings into the British Isles, which were still connected to continental Europe until around 6500 BC. The earliest traces of hominid activity are much older, however, possibly dating some 800,000 years back. Habitation during that time wasn't permanent, and Britain went through periods of abandonment, most likely due to harsh climate conditions.

Julius Caesar attempted to conquer Britain and failed. [1]

Initial attempts by the Romans to establish a foothold in Britain began in 55 and 54 BC as part of Julius Caesar's Gallic Wars. Caesar's expeditions failed to consolidate direct Roman control in Britain, but they paved the way for later conquests and were an important episode in overall British history. This was primarily due to the introduction of goods and trade that enriched the local rulers in the southern edges of Britain. Roman invasions resumed in earnest under Emperor Claudius in 43 AD. After a prolonged period of back-and-forth expansions and contractions as Rome vied with the native Britons, the Roman borders in Britain were solidified with the building of Hadrian's Wall, which was started in 122 and took about 6 years to finish. The wall, which stretches for 80 miles, was and still is located not far south of the present-day border between England and Scotland.

The first people recorded to have considered themselves English were the descendants of Germanic peoples who came to Britain from northern Europe, particularly during the Anglo-Saxon migrations. The Anglo-Saxons, a collection of Germanic tribes, sought to fill a vacuum left by the collapse of Roman rule, and they consolidated themselves in various parts of Britain from the 5th century onward. Centuries of inter-tribal conflict and fighting with the indigenous Britons ensued, giving rise and fall to numerous kingdoms and, eventually, the English national genesis.

Attempting to pinpoint when a particular nation began to perceive itself as such is always a contentious and thankless endeavor. The formation of England's national identity, in the broadest sense, can be regarded as a long process spawned by conflict and fusion between two primary groups. The first group, nowadays collectively referred to as Anglo-Saxons due to their eventual common identity, primarily included the Angles, Saxons, Jutes, and Frisians.

As these Germanic tribes settled, expanded, and consolidated their rule in the southern portion of Britain, they made contact with local Britons. These were mainly Celts who themselves had absorbed Roman influence by that point. The bulk of the settlement process most likely transpired between the mid-5th and early 7th centuries. The Germanic settlers dramatically changed the linguistic and cultural picture of what later became England, but they also absorbed Romano-British influence in the process. All of these processes would eventually contribute to the emergence of a new English identity, especially after the unification of England in the early 10th century, thanks to Edward the Elder and his son Athelstan.

William the Conqueror

From the very beginning of Anglo-Saxon dominion over England, there were others who had their hungry gaze set on the British Isles. The Norman Conquest in the 11th century was a major turning point in early English history that dramatically affected the subsequent historical course of the realm. William of Normandy played a central role in these events. Indeed, one of the most important 11th-century figures to rule over England was a foreigner, styled William the Conqueror not for his conquests on behalf of England but his conquest of it.

The Young Norman Duke, William II

William, also known as William the Bastard, was born around 1028 in Falaise, Duchy of Normandy, as an illegitimate child of Robert the Magnificent and his concubine, Herleva. Even though he was the recognized son of the Duke of Normandy, William's upbringing carried numerous difficulties. When the time came for Robert I of Normandy to be succeeded, his son was both young and illegitimate, making his ascension somewhat problematic. Further complicating the situation was the unstable state of Normandy at that time, with various Norman aristocrats vying for influence over young William and the realm.

The Normans originated from invading Vikings who settled in northern France around 911 when Rollo, the first ruler of these Norse settlers, was granted land by the Frankish king, Charles the Simple. William, just like his father, was a descendant of Rollo, with a clear lineage to the Vikings who came to Normandy more than a century earlier. Rollo was the first of the Vikings to agree to a religious conversion and pledge allegiance to the Frankish king, so by the time William was born, Normans had already taken on a life of their own in the new homeland.

William the Conqueror. '

Even though William wasn't a child born in wedlock, his mother was a well-situated woman whose father was a successful merchant with political connections. Herleva had two other sons, half-brothers to William, who also went on to play significant political and religious roles in the region. William himself would eventually get married somewhere between 1050 and 1053. His wife was Matilda of Flanders, descended from the powerful House of Flanders, whose County of Flanders played a distinguished role in the Low Countries until the late 18th century.

As the daughter of the Count of Flanders and a niece to Henry I of France, Matilda was a powerful woman, and her marriage to William consolidated a powerful alliance in the region. It would also be a fruitful marriage, as Matilda not only became the Duchess of Normandy and Queen of England but also birthed four sons and four or five daughters, according to different sources.

Despite his youth, his contemporaries described William as a formidable young man. One particularly flattering account that has been preserved comes from William of Poitiers, a Norman priest and chronicler of the subsequent Norman Conquest of England. He described William as a mighty horseman who could stand shoulder to shoulder with any adult, possessing great strength, a keen military mind, and a passion for justice. William of Poitiers clearly had an affinity toward the young duke, but his idealized account was likely based on truths that were evident at the time, given that his seal portrayed a knight mounted on a horse.

The duke's subsequent political career clearly illustrates that he was adept at political maneuvering, administration, and much more than just combat and military strategy. Another tidbit from William's personal life is that he was an avid hunter and conservationist, which his policies reflected both in Normandy and later in England. He enforced strict laws in forestry and hunting, going to great lengths to combat poaching.

William was only around seven to eight years old when his father, Robert, died in Anatolia in 1035. Despite his illegitimate birth, William's claim to become the new Duke of Normandy was facilitated by his father's public steps to make him his heir. Robert also made sure to obtain oaths of loyalty from his subordinate barons in advance, obligating them to respect his wishes. Some of the aristocrats had different plans, however, and Normandy was plunged into civil war when the young duke's guardian, Gilbert of Brionne, was murdered in 1040.

It took years for Duke William II, as he was known in Normandy, to subdue rebellious barons and establish a firm grip on power. His successes were in significant part owing to his numerous, powerful allies and their political and military support, not least of which came from Henry I, the King of the Franks at that time. It wasn't until 1047 that William and his allies were able to deal a decisive blow to the rebels, but fighting went on for several more years until a semblance of stability returned.

William essentially grew up in constant war, which turned him into a menacing military figure and one of the most renowned military strategists in Europe at that time. Such an upbringing also made him ruthless, and the duke rarely shied away from brutality and terror to keep his enemies in line.

Conquest and Rule Over England

By the 1050s, the power of William and the Duchy of Normandy had reached unprecedented heights. Some of the nobles who had once supported him began to look upon William with mistrust and fear. Chief among them was William's once key supporter, Henry I, the King of the Franks. Henry joined forces with other aristocrats who felt that it was time to put a leash on William's growing power, including William's uncle, William of Arques.

None of this would be enough to bring down the duke, however, and he would ultimately prevail over all the local contenders as well as the king's forces assembled from across France. Having failed to bring William under control, the king died in 1060 and was succeeded by his underage son. The boy's guardian was none other than Robert of Flanders, William's father-in-law. With his power unchecked and the contenders in Normandy and its continental neighborhood essentially pacified, William could now shift his gaze across the water.

William's decision to cross the English Channel and conquer England was based on a claim to the English throne, which was unstable and heavily contested at the time. Other ambitious men laid the same claim, but William set forth a case that rested on familial relations. In particular, he emphasized his relation to Edward the Confessor, who ruled England between 1042 and 1066 and was the grandson of Count Richard I of Normandy, who was William's great-grandfather. William and his Norman supporters then started spreading what was essentially a rumor, saying that Edward had made William his heir via a verbal promise some years earlier.

Whether that past promise was made or not, Edward would name an Anglo-Saxon military leader, Harold Godwinson, as his heir on his deathbed in 1066. William had other obstacles, too. For one, the Duke of Normandy was a vassal to the King of France, so William didn't have the authority to mount such a massive military campaign on a whim, no matter how powerful his duchy was within the wider kingdom. Politics aside, such an undertaking would have required an enormous army made up of forces from across France, requiring at least the support of many barons, if not the king himself.

The barons, however, could be enticed and bought with grand promises of spoils and power if an invasion of England was to turn out successful. Through clever politics and perhaps his fearsome reputation, William was able to gradually recruit a number of nobles to his cause. He also obtained the Pope's blessing to invade, thanks to the Papacy's conflict with the Archbishop of Canterbury in England. With religious, military, and political winds now at his back, William began his preparations during the summer of 1066, a few months after Harold II Godwinson was crowned King of England.

The invasion began at an opportune moment because Harold II already had to fight off a Norwegian invasion several weeks before William landed in Sussex on September 25, 1066. The initial invasion force numbered no more than 8,000 men, about a quarter of which consisted of cavalrymen. The size of the English army that went to meet them is difficult to ascertain, but it likely wasn't much larger, probably due to attrition from fighting the Norwegians. The decisive moment in the invasion came during the Battle of Hastings on October 14, pitting Anglo-Saxon infantry against William's cavalry charges and archers.

The course of the battle was uncertain at times. According to English accounts, Harold II's infantry managed to inflict significant losses on Norman cavalry units, which even started to flee at one point. William's military skills and exemplary leadership helped him turn the units back into battle and, with the support of his archers, mount multiple devastating charges against the English. The Norman duke also used other tactics, such as feigned retreats, to lure English infantry into preferred kill zones. William the Conqueror was ultimately victorious, inflicting heavy casualties on the defenders and killing Harold II in the process. He then waited for reinforcements from Normandy and pressed on to London with a fresh and refitted army, where he would be crowned William I of England on Christmas 1066.

The job was far from done; however, the most powerful man on both sides of the Channel had to put down revolts, which went on for five years. Just as in Normandy, ruthless suppression against rebels and strategic distribution of land and wealth among his loyal nobles bore fruit, and William I was able to gradually consolidate his hold over England. He also reshuffled the clergy by bringing in Norman bishops. William was so successful in establishing his administration that he was able to rule in his absence. He routinely went back to France in his capacity as Duke of Normandy while leaving others in charge of England. The most trusted of his managers were his half-brother Odo of Bayeux and close confidant William FitzOsbern, earls of Kent and Hereford, respectively.

William's subsequent rule as both the King of England and Duke of Normandy was wrought with many additional challenges. He had to subdue unruly nobles and repel foreign raids in both realms, which he continued to do with success until his luck finally ran out in 1077 when he suffered a defeat in Brittany. Even his eldest son, Robert, rebelled shortly afterward, bringing additional defeats at the hands of a son seemingly just as adept at warfare as the father. The two eventually reconciled, and Robert helped fend off Scottish raids into England in 1079.

One of the best testaments to William's skills as an administrator was the Domesday Book, which was a document containing a meticulous survey of land ownership across England. This attention to detail established a more complex feudal system than England had seen prior to Norman rule, sowing the seeds of further administrative development for a long time to come. The survey contained in the Domesday Book was a document without precedent during the Middle Ages in terms of its detail and meticulousness. It is preserved to this day as one of the most critical pieces of William's legacy.

William the Conqueror died on September 9, 1087, under unclear circumstances, either succumbing to illness or an injury. The Anglo-Saxon Chronicle, known for its anti-Norman stance, described William as wise, pious, and stronger than his predecessors. It also noted his penchant for justice, gentle conduct toward the virtuous, and cruelty toward his enemies.

Henry II

The rule of Henry II, which lasted between 1154 and 1189, came about in the aftermath of a period of strife and civil war known in English historiography as "The Anarchy." A new dynasty and undoubtedly one of England's greatest monarchs were thus born of chaos and disarray. Before and at the beginning of Henry II's rule, conflict around succession was a problem that had plagued both England and Normandy for some time. Henry II was able to usher in a level of stability that allowed the realm not just to consolidate and develop but also to influence the whole world in some significant ways, particularly regarding the rule of law.

Henry II. [*]

Henry of Anjou

Just like William the Conqueror, Henry was born in what is now northwestern France, more precisely, Le Mans. He was born Henry of Anjou on March 5, 1133, inheriting his initial title from his father Geoffrey, who was the Count of Anjou at that time. Henry's mother, Matilda, had acquired the impressive title of empress after marrying

Henry V, the Holy Roman Emperor who died in 1125. Matilda was also the daughter of Henry I of England, who was one of the sons of William the Conqueror. She married Geoffrey in 1128 after the death of her first husband.

The family from which Henry II came was referred to by others as Plantagenet, and it produced a number of kings, including Henry II himself, Richard the Lionheart, and King John. Because they all came from Anjou, these monarchs also became known as the Angevins, which is why the dynasty that Henry II would establish in England became known as Plantagenet-Angevin.

Henry showed great promise from a very young age and would receive an education that allowed him to master multiple languages. He was described as intelligent and handsome, as well as ambitious and highly spirited. Far from being just a medieval bookworm, Henry also had a formidable physical presence, being fierce both in body and spirit. With his noble upbringing, numerous natural blessings, and the many perks of being high-born, the young noble seemed to have always been meant for greatness. The lands and titles he inherited from his father were impressive but were merely the overture for his many later achievements.

Even though he had already tasted victory and became the Duke of Normandy by that time, Henry's life took a significant turn when he married Eleanor of Aquitaine in 1152. Eleanor had previously married Louis VII of France, but this marriage was annulled in 1152 for failing to produce any viable heirs. Eleanor was an incredibly powerful woman, having already acquired immense wealth and influence when she married the ambitious Norman Duke. She was much more than a clever politician or financial manager, though, as she dabbled in art, literature, and much more. The influence she was able to exert on the overall situation in medieval Europe was truly astounding for a woman, making her one of the most revered female nobles in European history.

With his many gifts, ambitions, and such a powerful woman at his side, Henry eventually came to dominate most of France, and he would soon set his sights on the English throne as well. England was particularly vulnerable at the time, experiencing a power vacuum due to the ongoing succession crisis. The crisis was mainly the result of King Henry I's lack of male heirs after his reign had ended in 1135. Henry I had hoped that his daughter Matilda could take over, making her his heir and having his nobles pledge loyalty.

The arrangement quickly fell apart after the king's death because many barons had no intention of being vassals to a woman, much less one from Anjou. Soon thereafter, the nobles shifted their support, making Stephen of Blois, a man of immense wealth, the next King of England. Matilda would not back down from her legitimate inheritance without a fight, however, leading to years of civil war. The English nobility was largely split between Stephen of Blois and Matilda, and the conflict entailed many ups and downs for both sides. The Anarchy would last roughly between 1138 and 1153, wreaking havoc upon England and making the realm ripe for the picking by the time Matilda's son Henry grew in strength and influence.

Henry II of England

Henry's initial attempts to intervene militarily in the civil war in England, which started in 1147, ended in failure. The second attempt in 1149 even secured assistance from Scotland's David I, but yet again, the invading forces were defeated by Stephen. It was clear that Henry would need to be patient and spend more time building up his forces if he was to succeed, so he postponed the third invasion to 1153. This invasion also came at a time of personal weakness for Stephen, as he was grieving following his wife's death.

Whether it was Stephen's emotional exhaustion or Henry's shrewd diplomacy, the two sides managed to resolve the issue through negotiations. Stephen would remain king until he died, but he would name Henry as the heir to his throne. The Treaty of Wallingford was generally well-received by the nobles, who saw Henry as a competent man and a fitting candidate. They were also tired of the civil war, as was everyone else in England. Henry II was crowned king on December 19, 1154, at Westminster Abbey, introducing unity and peace that had been absent in England for a long time.

The years of anarchy had brought England to the edge of dissolution, with many unruly barons exploiting the breakdown in central power to introduce their own currencies, expand at will, impose their own rules on the peasantry, and build castles illegally. The early phase of Henry II's rule was all about resolving these issues and restoring order. Henry II thus began one of the most crucial aspects of his reign, which was legal reform.

These efforts were embodied in the Assize of Clarendon, which was a major legal act of 1166 and transformed English law forever. The era of common law thus began, replacing obsolete systems like trial by battle with trial by jury, consisting of 12 men. The trials would be held at courts sanctioned by the crown, also known as the assize courts. These reforms paved the way for basic legal systems that would spread all over the world.

Henry II also had to restore security to England's borders, sorting out neighboring realms that had been launching opportunistic attacks against England during The Anarchy. Henry accomplished this with diplomacy – also applying military force when necessary. England's influence over neighboring Wales, Scotland, and Ireland increased significantly during Henry II's reign, and the Pope eventually recognized the power of the English crown over the entirety of Britain and Ireland.

Henry II's fruitful reign wasn't without controversy, however. One of the worst incidents of Henry II's life was the killing of Thomas Becket, his friend, chancellor, and Archbishop of Canterbury. The breakdown in their relationship was the result of Henry II's growing conflict with the Church because Becket felt that the king was interfering in its affairs, unjustly taxing it, and trying to exert state control over the sacred institution. While Henry II had become deeply frustrated with Becket by 1170, the Archbishop's murder might have been the result of a misunderstanding between Henry and his knights. The outrageous killing, which was perpetrated while Becket was praying in the Canterbury Cathedral, sent shock waves across the realm and beyond.

Becket's death landed the king in hot water with the Pope and also sowed the seeds of later rebellions, especially those by his sons and his estranged wife Eleanor, which began in earnest from 1173 onward. The initial rebellion that year was started by the king's eldest son, Henry, and Eleanor, who allied with a few nobles who held grudges against the king over what had happened to Becket. Personal ambitions also played their parts, of course, and the king's list of enemies snowballed, eventually including such influential figures as Sir William Marshal and Philip II of France. Henry II was able to put down the early rebellions, but the 1180s brought further challenges. He was ultimately forced to come to an agreement in 1189, giving concessions to the king in France and naming his third and previously disloyal son Richard as his successor in England. The king died in the summer of that year, surrounded by people whom he felt had betrayed him.

Chapter 2: Thomas Becket and Henry VIII: Church, Crown, and Conflict

It could be said that there are at least some patterns that human history has followed across the world. However, different nations have also put their own spin on things, and their histories have revolved around certain themes that people have come to associate with those nations. England has had a number of such themes, and one of them was the monarchy's conflict and subsequent break with the Catholic Church in Rome. Thomas Becket and his unfortunate falling out with Henry II of England was an earlier example of these frictions. The 16th-century reign of Henry VIII, however, serves as a more famous example.

Henry VIII. '

Thomas Becket

Thomas Becket was a consequential figure in 12th-century England due to the political and clerical roles he played, but it was his death that cemented him as a significant historical figure. This legacy took on even more meaning in the subsequent centuries and within the context of other, more dramatic clashes between England and the Pope. Had things ended with Becket's death, perhaps his life would have been little more than a historical episode.

However, the fact and manner of his death, along with the shock waves it would send throughout the land, would benefit immensely from a historical perspective. Amid the later events of the Reformation and other religious strife in England, many historians and onlookers from Becket's future would start seeing that his life and death were perhaps a foreshadowing of things they were witnessing in their time. Nowadays, the whole Becket affair resembles a stepping stone in a long chain of events that precipitated the final break between England and the Papacy.

The King's Man

According to different sources, Thomas Becket was born in 1118, 1119, or 1120, but there is general agreement that his birthday was December 21, which is also the feast day of St. Thomas the Apostle. He is also known as Thomas of London and Saint Thomas of Canterbury, owed to his subsequent veneration as a saint and martyr by the Church in Rome. Centuries later, he was also venerated by the Anglican Communion.

Thomas was born into a wealthy merchant family in London, where his father made his fortune by supplying the royal court with wine. From a young age, Thomas was raised in an environment of learning and great promise, starting his education at a monastery belonging to the Merton Priory in London. He only spent a short while at this school, a theme that he would soon repeat in Paris, Bologna, and other places.

Given Becket's subsequent conflict with Henry II and his dramatic end, his career started off in a completely different, even opposite, direction. This was despite the fact that he began his work years as a clerk of the Archbishop of Canterbury in 1146. A few years later, he would move further up the ladder by becoming an archdeacon. Not much is known about how Thomas Becket performed in these functions, but his successes can be extrapolated from the kind of company he would acquire. Already in the early 1150s, Becket made the king's acquaintance and would be appointed Lord Chancellor in early 1155.

The chancellor's position didn't hold too much weight when Becket first took it, but Henry II, already a good friend of Becket, enabled him to run things as he saw fit. It seems that Becket had found himself right at home in his new post and was able to significantly expand the role, influence, and efficiency of the chancellor seat. It didn't take long until Becket's office started to resemble what might be considered a prime minister nowadays, holding significant sway over other ministries of government. Thomas was also trusted with the king's children, frequently tutoring Henry the Young King and acting as a guardian for other nobles. The friendly relationship between Thomas and Henry II also extended into personal life, and they even found time to engage in hobbies like hunting together.

During this early stage of his career, Thomas was almost a right-hand man to the king, often doing his bidding even at the expense of the Church, in sharp contrast to his later destiny. In his position as chancellor, Becket made sure that the Church was paying copious amounts in taxes, which were used to fund his king's war efforts. He took on a rather negative reputation throughout England because of this, particularly among the clergy. Not only that, but Becket also enriched himself, and he made no secret of it, living an extravagant lifestyle with plenty of servants, expensive food, and other luxuries.

Part of his wealth came from money, but he was made even richer thanks to the many properties bestowed upon him as a reward for his loyal service to the English throne. He even had what was essentially a private army consisting of hundreds of knights. All of this extravagance and indulgence would become largely forgotten after his death and his final years, as Becket's life took an astonishing turn.

Conflict and an Outrage for the Ages

It is impossible to know when precisely the seeds of doubt were planted within Thomas Becket, but somewhere along the way, a radical change would send his life and everything around him into a spin. However, there is some question about how radical or earnest that change had been, as Becket might have made a conscious choice to change his ways in accordance with his new job. Indeed, the eventual clash can be seen as the result of a significant miscalculation by Henry II when he decided to appoint Becket as the Archbishop of Canterbury in 1162.

Around this time, Henry II had made it his mission to bring the Church down a few pegs on the power ladder and exert more state control over the clergy. Legal jurisdiction was a particularly heated issue between the English crown and the Roman Church, with the Church demanding a high degree of autonomy or outright independence to enforce its own laws on its extensive lands how it saw fit. Completely annulling the king's authority in such disputes and, in some cases, even transferring authority to the Pope – technically a foreign center of power – was

Thomas Becket. [s]

something that Henry II couldn't tolerate. Despite the separation of state and clergy, the king did have the power to appoint the Archbishop of Canterbury, an important clerical authority in England. Henry II could hardly think of a better man for the job than Becket, who was a great friend with a long record of being tough on the Church.

As the archbishop, Becket started out as a controversial figure among the clergy because he initially retained much of his previous secular lifestyle. This changed after about a year, when he suddenly started foregoing his luxuries and devoting himself to religion, also resigning from his post as chancellor. It is impossible to ascertain whether Thomas had experienced a genuine change of character or was simply trying to excel at his new job, but within a short while, he became a devoted protector of the Church. As Becket began to buck the king's attempts to strengthen the state's hold over the Church, Henry II realized that the man he had appointed to help him subdue the clergy had, in fact, become its greatest protector.

Things escalated very quickly from that point on, with Henry and Thomas becoming staunch rivals in a very public manner. They would constantly try to smear each other's reputation, spreading rumors, raising serious allegations of corruption, and much more.

A major step in the escalation came in 1164 as Henry II began his massive legal reforms in England, taking the opportunity to slash the independence of the Church as much as he could. Thomas Becket resisted these attempts and refused to swear allegiance, but he lacked the support he needed from the rest of the clergy. Henry II was a powerful monarch, and many religious figures realized it was time to cut their losses and make compromises. As a result, Becket was officially held in contempt of the crown and forced to flee England, settling in France with all his properties back home taken by the state.

The king probably hoped that this exile would be the end of the ordeal, and for six years, it was. Becket returned in late 1170 thanks to the initiative of the Papacy. Upon his return, he and Henry seemed to have reconciled for a short while, but nothing had fundamentally changed in their attitudes, goals, behaviors, and politics. The conflict quickly resumed when Becket began lustrating the bishops who didn't help him six years earlier, excommunicating them from the Church.

Such insolence immediately sent shockwaves through the royal court, backing the mighty king into a corner. The subsequent assassination of Becket was most likely unintended on the king's part. History writes that, at a moment of desperation, Henry II uttered a fateful sentence, lamenting, "Will no one rid me of this turbulent priest?" He wasn't alone when he made this exclamation, and his subordinates who heard him interpreted this sentence as an order to get rid of Becket. Four knights initially tried to arrest the archbishop in his home but were forced to back down by his supporters. Sometime later, they confronted Becket yet again, but this time they were intoxicated. They barged into the Canterbury Cathedral in the middle of service, demanding that Thomas turn himself in. After his repeated refusal to surrender, things escalated, and the archbishop was brutally slashed by multiple swords, verbally pledging his life to Christ and the Church as he died, welcoming his death.

The seemingly reborn, once extravagant former politician immediately became a martyr. His outrageous murder precipitated such an intense firestorm of controversy that the king spent some time in Ireland for his own safety. It eventually came to light that Henry II wasn't personally responsible, so his punishment consisted of little more than a walk of penance in the cathedral where Becket died. He was able to avoid excommunication, but the Roman Church used the opportunity to force the king to make concessions in their legal disputes regarding Henry's controversial Constitutions of Clarendon. He would later enact major legal reforms through his Assize of Clarendon, but the Church retained its independence.

Becket was canonized in 1173 and was henceforth known as Saint Thomas of Canterbury. Henry II's otherwise glorious reign had been tarnished forever, and it seemed that the Church had won a significant victory. However, this victory was to be temporary as the seeds of conflict had been sown deep, and the friction with the English crown would persist for centuries to come. The controversy of Thomas Becket was indicative of radical disagreements that were sure to crop up again and led to a much more significant split between the royal and ecclesiastical centers of power.

Henry VIII

The extent to which Henry VIII was a controversial figure depends on who is passing the judgment. In the Catholic world, he was looked at with disdain, and many of his actions were considered abominable. The conflict initially revolved around Henry's desire to dissolve his marriage in his desperate pursuit of a male heir, but the clash with Rome evolved into a much more dramatic controversy with historical repercussions. Beyond his conflict with the Church, Henry VIII was a formidable, eccentric figure in his time, and his eventful reign left a significant historical impact. His reign between 1509 and 1547 was decisive in bringing the Reformation to England, marking the culmination of a centuries-long drift.

A King Set for Success

Henry VIII was born into the House of Tudor on June 28, 1491, in Greenwich and would become the second king this dynasty would produce in England. The origins of the House of Tudor can be found in the Wars of the Roses, a famous period of dynastic strife that lasted between 1455 and 1487. During that time, the old House of Plantagenet had split into two warring branches, the houses of Lancaster and York.

Even though they ultimately prevailed, the Lancasters suffered significant damage that put an end to their male line of succession. This was how their allied House of Tudor, newly formed and led by Henry Tudor, inherited the claim to the throne. Henry Tudor was crowned Henry VII in 1485, and he made great strides in stabilizing and strengthening the monarchy before the birth of his son Henry in 1491.

England left the Middle Ages as a stable, unified monarchy thanks to the responsible leadership of Henry VII. Henry VIII's father was also a careful spender with a fine mind for economics, which helped England strengthen its finances. Henry VIII, crowned in 1509, inherited an all-around solid kingdom to look after. As a young man, Henry VIII was already an imposing figure in both stature and character. He was well over six feet tall, recorded as 1.9 meters, and he was known for his athleticism.

Henry excelled at archery and horse riding, making him a formidable participant in his father's various tournaments. He also dabbled in sports such as tennis. Henry didn't neglect his mind and spirit either, taking time to write poetry, study theology, and compose music. These endeavors were more than just a show of noble sophistication for the young prince, as he was widely known for his intelligence. Tall, athletic, red-haired, and intelligent, Henry found it easy to charm everyone he met. However, he had a darker side, which featured occasional outbursts of anger. It would seem that, in the course of his reign, Henry VIII would gradually stray further and further into that darkness, becoming prone to paranoia, malice, and cruelty.

The "Great Matter" and Its Consequences

The real saga began with Henry VIII's marriage to Catherine of Aragon. This was his first and by far longest marriage, starting a couple of months after his coronation in 1509 and lasting until 1533. It would prove to be a severe mismatch marred by tragedy throughout the years. The royal couple would have a total of six children, five of whom passed away as infants. The only child of Catherine who survived was Mary, born in 1516.

Catherine of Aragon. *

Henry's one true goal was to acquire a male heir, and it was increasingly clear that this was impossible in his current marriage. In 1519, he actually fathered a son, Henry FitzRoy, who became the Duke of Richmond and Somerset, but FitzRoy was an illegitimate son of a mistress. After a while, Henry VIII decided to embark upon an extensive search for a replacement, eventually finding Anne Boleyn. However, getting a divorce was no simple matter for a 16th-century monarch, and the whole endeavor would come to be known as "the king's great matter." Henry needed to ask Pope Clement VII for an official annulment of his previous marriage, so he sent a letter to Rome, stating his case in great detail.

The king argued that his lack of a male heir was God's way of punishing him for marrying the wife of his deceased older brother, Arthur, citing Leviticus 20:21. This part of the Old Testament states that he who marries his brother's wife commits an act of impurity and dishonors his brother, dooming his marriage to childlessness. The argument was strong, but the Pope had political reasons to reject his request regardless due to Catherine's familial relations with the Holy Roman Emperor, Charles V of Spain.

The Pope still presented a religious argument for his reluctance, stating that the marriage between Catherine and Arthur was unlikely to have been consummated due to their young age. The Church also sent an investigator to determine the facts and try to mediate between Henry and his wife, who had no intention of giving up her seat as queen. The whole affair got very ugly in short order. Mediation attempts failed, and Henry eventually resorted to keeping his wife locked away at various locations away from him and Anne Boleyn, with whom he was now living. The two eventually had a daughter, Elizabeth, born in 1533. Consumed by his pursuit of a male heir, Henry VIII could hardly realize that Elizabeth would one day become one of the most successful English rulers.

From then on, Henry was committed to annulling his marriage to Catherine by any means necessary. A protracted standoff with the Church ensued, culminating with the Act of Supremacy on November 28, 1534, which proclaimed that the King of England was the highest worldly authority and the head of the Church, with only God above him. The act changed England's religious, ecclesiastical, and political landscape forever. This was how the Reformation came to England within the context of the broader current in Europe.

The Dissolution of the Monasteries Act of 1536 was the next big step in the Parliament, enabling Henry VIII to seize monastic estates to redistribute as he saw fit. The entire episode sparked outrage across the Catholic world and even within England, but few dared to speak up against Henry lest they end up like a number of abbots who were hanged for their protests. Nonetheless, many were happy to see the Reformation arrive due to the not-so-rare perception that the Roman Church had become decadent, and so England eventually settled into its new destiny.

Henry VIII's infamous streak of marriages continued less than three years after he had married Anne Boleyn, whom he executed by beheading in 1536 at the Tower of London after accusing her of adultery, witchcraft, and other grave offenses. It is likely that there was little veracity to these charges, however, as Henry was unhappy with the marriage and had already expressed interest in his next wife, Jane Seymour. The king's third marriage would finally produce a son, Edward, born in 1537. All accounts indicate that Jane was the one wife whom Henry truly loved, but she died shortly after the birth of Edward. His following two marriages, to Anne of Cleves and Catherine Howard, were also short-lived, with the first ending in divorce and the second, yet again, with the wife's beheading. The king's sixth and final wife, Catherine Parr, was the only one to outlive Henry VIII, who died on January 28, 1547.

Beyond his marriages and the fact that he had separated the English Church from the Pope, the reign of Henry VIII involved other controversies. In contrast to his father, Henry VIII was infamous for his irresponsible spending, most of which went to his many military campaigns and lavish palaces. He had over 60 houses, all of which were the picture of luxury and extravagance.

When Henry VIII died, his male heir was still a child. Nine-year-old Edward VI of England inherited a financially unstable kingdom that was still reeling from the religious outrages and schisms initiated by his father. As tumultuous and controversial as his reign was, Henry VIII's legacy and historical weight are enormous. Between 1534 and 1546, he established two major pillars of the great power that his kingdom would later become – the Church of England and the Royal Navy.

Chapter 3: Elizabeth I and the Rise of English Naval Power

Volumes could be written about the monumental 44-year reign of Elizabeth I. For a monarch who was technically never meant to sit on the throne, Elizabeth I crushed all expectations and strengthened her country in ways that ensured her legacy reverberated through the ages. Almost two centuries before Queen Victoria, Elizabeth I was the first queen to have an era of English history named after her, known as the Elizabethan era, also referred to as the Golden Age of England.

Elizabeth I was the first queen to have an era of English history named after her. [7]

Elizabeth I successfully outmaneuvered and defeated numerous enemies during her reign, including foreign and domestic ones. Through her victories over some of the most formidable world powers at that time, such as Spain, she successfully protected England and cemented it as a consequential geopolitical player. Elizabeth I's England bloomed politically, militarily, culturally, and artistically. By the time Elizabeth was done, England was ready to take the world by storm and compete with the most powerful colonial superpowers of the day.

Elizabeth's Unforeseen Greatness

One of the fascinating facts about Elizabeth I is that she had a fairly rough start for someone born to royalty. She came into a wretched marriage between Henry VIII and his second wife, Anne Boleyn. Not only did her father kill her mother, but she would also have to suffer the repercussions of being declared an illegitimate child after Henry annulled his marriage with Anne. Growing up in the chaos of Henry's many marital escapades and indiscretions and his other children, she had few prospects in the royal family, but history had different plans.

From Illegitimacy to the English Throne

Elizabeth was born at Greenwich Palace on September 7, 1533, the only child of Henry VIII's infamous second marriage. She was most likely conceived while Henry VIII was still embattled with the Roman Church over his attempts to annul his first marriage and marry Anne. However, this had little bearing on Elizabeth's subsequent illegitimacy since she would be born months after Henry and Anne were formally married in early 1533. Elizabeth was merely a first attempt as far as Henry was concerned.

Even though he acknowledged his love for his daughter, Henry still expected Anne to produce a male heir. Unfortunately for him and Anne, their subsequent attempts resulted in three miscarriages. Elizabeth was less than three years old when this marriage came to a gruesome end in May of 1536. After Henry had Anne executed at the Tower of London, Elizabeth found herself becoming an illegitimate child overnight. She would still live with the family, but her rights as a member of royalty were annulled with the marriage that had produced her. The king's subsequent marriage with Jane Seymour soon produced a male heir when Edward was born in October 1537. Now that the king had finally gotten the male successor he had sought for so long, Elizabeth and the rest of the king's children were entirely sidelined in terms of eventual succession.

For Elizabeth, things finally started looking up when Henry VIII married his sixth wife, Catherine Parr, in the summer of 1543. Catherine took custody of Henry's children from previous marriages, and she made sure that the children were properly cared for. Young Elizabeth began receiving an extensive education in all sorts of fields, including theology, history, philosophy, arts, and everything else a young royal was expected to study. She also started learning multiple languages and was coached in the art of rhetoric, which would prove a valuable skill during her time on the throne. Elizabeth also likely had a natural knack for oration and writing.

When Elizabeth's father died in 1547, her younger half-brother Edward became king of his father's financially troubled realm. Over the next six years, in which the severely underage Edward tried to fill his father's shoes, Elizabeth seems to have expressed no interest in power. She generally avoided the affairs of the state and lived a quiet life in Hertfordshire. King Edward VI died in 1553 when he was just 15 years old, and since Henry had no other male heirs, the eldest daughter, Mary, sat on the throne. Mary I's reign lasted until 1558, which was a tumultuous period due to the queen's Catholic faith. She sought to reverse the Reformation process, annulling laws but not shying away from brutal repression. Her violent methods, not least of which was her propensity for incinerating Protestants at the stake, earned her the infamous moniker of Bloody Mary.

Her brutality and the fact that she married Prince Philip of Spain, a country widely perceived as a significant rival to England, quickly made Mary I unpopular. The increasing dislike of Mary I's policies culminated in the 1554 Wyatt Rebellion. It's unclear whether or not Elizabeth had any hand in these events, but it was speculated and rumored that the rebels were planning to install her as the new queen. Even though Elizabeth had made it a point to stay out of politics, Mary I heeded the growing suspicions of those around her and eventually had Elizabeth arrested. Luckily, after a period of house arrest, the half-sisters were able to move past their conflict and heal the relationship.

The Elizabethan Era

In November of 1558, Mary I succumbed to what is thought to have been stomach cancer, ending a short and turbulent reign. As she had no children, it suddenly became clear that Elizabeth was next in the line of succession. Her coronation took place on January 15, 1559, and although it was an opulent ceremony, it marked the beginning of a reign over a troubled monarchy. Financial problems dating back to Henry VIII had deteriorated by Elizabeth's time, and she had to contend with political instability and territorial losses in France. To make matters worse, there was no shortage of rivals and enemies, both foreign and domestic. At 25 years old, Elizabeth I was a young queen, but what she lacked in experience and skills was compensated by wisdom and self-awareness. Elizabeth wisely appointed capable, vetted counselors such as Lord William Cecil to offset her shortcomings in a fragile country. Another major asset was Sir Francis Walsingham, appointed Secretary of State and essentially acting as a spymaster.

Sir Francis Walsingham.[8]

Elizabeth quickly found that she would have to cleverly navigate and maneuver through a male-dominated world. She knew she had to be cunning but also decisive and assertive, and she would get that point across very promptly. Elizabeth was able to strike a delicate balance between a domineering independence and an ability to heed valuable advice from her counselors. Much of the policy-making process during her reign boiled down to members of her cabinet having to make tremendous efforts to convince her that their ideas had merit. After intense scrutiny by the queen, the best suggestions would make it into policy.

Elizabeth I was also very analytical and a realist, knowing perfectly well when she should cut her losses. This was how she managed to avoid the pitfalls of fruitless territorial ambitions in France and Scotland, which had bogged down many of her predecessors. Putting the realm first and paying little mind to the power of her own House of Tudor, she turned out to be a careful and calculated spender, which helped finally put the kingdom's finances back on track.

One of the defining characteristics of Elizabeth's reign was her refusal to get married. This was a point of disagreement between the queen and her devoted advisors, who felt that she should have at least one heir to ensure a smooth succession. Despite their counsel, Elizabeth remained steadfast in her decision to remain unwed. Publicly, she professed that she was married to her country, and she certainly played the part with her endless devotion to her duties on a daily basis.

However, there has been quite a bit of speculation among historians on whether or not Elizabeth had other reasons for her aversion toward marriage. Her father's disastrous marital escapades and Mary I's loss of reputation due to her marriage to a Spaniard possibly had some effect on Elizabeth. Furthermore, a lack of suitors was never a problem for Elizabeth, as she had received many highly enticing marriage proposals from powerful men both from England and abroad.

The queen's public image might also have played a part, at least later in life, as she had come to be known as the Virgin Queen. This public perception sometimes bordered on deification, as Elizabeth was often looked upon as a figure akin to the Virgin Mary. Still, it is entirely possible that Elizabeth went through several private relationships since it was no secret that she had affection for many men over the years, including one of her closest advisors, Robert Dudley.

Queen Elizabeth I was also known for her moderate approach to religious matters in England. She restored her father's steps toward Reformation, but she also exercised a great tolerance for Catholics. Extremists on both sides didn't look kindly upon the queen, but the silent masses generally approved of her approach. Elizabeth did try to promote Protestantism in staunchly Catholic Ireland, but this endeavor proved mostly fruitless.

Elizabeth demonstrated her capacity for violence and harsh action in her very high-profile conflict with Mary, Queen of Scots. Mary was Elizabeth's cousin through her father's sister, Margaret Tudor, and she became something of a champion for the Catholic cause in England. The conflict began when Mary returned from her exile in France and was met with strong opposition from the Protestant-majority of Scotland. The internal conflict forced Mary to abdicate her throne in 1567, after which she had to leave the northern kingdom. Mary met the same cold welcome in England, where Elizabeth preemptively incarcerated her. At that time, Elizabeth was faced with a Catholic rebellion in the north, which she crushed with her armies before hanging 900 men of the rebel army.

The Ridolfi Catholic plot of 1571 was another major test for Elizabeth. It was uncovered that the Duke of Norfolk had plotted to overthrow and assassinate Elizabeth with the help of the Spanish before installing Mary as the new queen. The duke was arrested and promptly executed in 1572, but Elizabeth refused to kill Mary despite the parliament's incessant requests in the 1580s. When an investigation by Francis Walsingham revealed that Mary had never abandoned her designs toward the throne and was, in fact, plotting with Philip of Spain to have the Spanish invade England, Elizabeth finally signed off on her execution in 1587.

Apart from such intrigues, the Elizabethan era was a time in which English culture and art blossomed in every way. The Theatre, which was London's first theater and playhouse, was established in 1576. Also during this era, the illustrious William Shakespeare began working, publishing historical plays such as Romeo and Juliet in 1593. Christopher Marlowe and Ben Jonson also left their marks during this time. The impact of these epoch-defining artistic breakthroughs cannot be overstated, as it is clearly and powerfully felt to this very day. However, as valuable as artistic and cultural legacy is, nothing could have changed the world as profoundly and directly as the events that would transpire on the seas.

The Birth of a Maritime Superpower

The 16th century wasn't the first time England had engaged in naval combat, of course, but it was undoubtedly a decisive era that turned English naval power into the colossus it would later become. Henry VIII was the monarch who officially founded the Royal Navy and established the foundations of its later development, but it was during Elizabeth I's reign that this investment would indeed start paying dividends. The naval power of England, which evolved into the Kingdom of Great Britain in 1707, was perhaps the critical pillar of the monarchy's global expansion in the Age of Exploration and beyond.

Naval Expansion under Elizabeth I

After the historic naval breakthroughs of the 15th century, such as the fabled exploits of Columbus and Vespucci, it was becoming increasingly clear that the future belonged to the explorer. By the time of Elizabeth I, major European powers were making great strides in this field, with colonies cropping up in the New World. The writing was on the wall, and Elizabeth knew that if England was to compete and even survive, the monarchy would have to commit.

Spain had already gotten a significant head start, so the queen began investing in England's naval capabilities and encouraging exploration. She did this by investing in the Royal Navy and in private enterprise, which was to be one of the core pillars of English imperial expansion. The Royal Navy was to ensure the security of England and its waters while private interests, encouraged and supported by the queen, would push the frontiers across the seas. This was the birth of England's Protestant privateers, who began their quests for wealth and glory in the 1560s and would soon start spreading all over the world.

Francis Drake was one of the queen's most prolific and legendary privateers, as well as the first Englishman who circumnavigated the world. The third overall navigator to accomplish this remarkable feat, Drake managed to do it in a single expedition that started in 1577 and ended in 1580. Prior to this expedition, Drake was exploring Panama. John Hawkins was another distinguished privateer who explored Spain's West Indies and West Africa in the 1560s, which was how England came into contact with and joined the lucrative Atlantic slave trade.

Francis Drake. [9]

All of these private endeavors were sanctioned and fully supported by the crown, which registered companies and provided them with charters. The privateers and their companies enjoyed significant freedom and discretionary autonomy, allowing them to establish a presence in areas they deemed profitable. They would then obtain exclusive rights in those areas as long as they would give the crown its due share of the profits. This was how the legendary, albeit infamous, East India Company came to be after it had secured its exclusive trading rights in the Indian Ocean in 1600. The queen's system was a self-perpetuating craze for exploration, trade, wealth, personal glory, and the Protestant cause. The diehard Catholic Spaniards were the perfect enemy and competitor, as would be Portugal a while later.

During their voyages, English privateers frequently clashed with the Spaniards, sometimes as a result of accidental encounters but often as part of raiding and piracy. The privateers plundered valuable goods, exotic items, gold, silver, arms, ships, and slaves whenever they could. The privateers intercepted ships, pillaged colonies, and even assaulted Spanish naval bases, partly motivated by personal gain and partly encouraged by policy.

The Humbling of Spain

Complementary to privateer raids were Elizabeth's efforts to stoke the flames of rebellion among Protestants ruled by Spain wherever she could. This was nothing new or particularly outrageous, though, as Spain had been doing the same with Catholics in England and the wider British Isles, on top of plotting to invade and overthrow Elizabeth. To that effect, the Spanish Netherlands and France were important targets for English interference. England's efforts to provoke rebellions against Philip II began in earnest in the 1570s.

These subversions, the 1587 execution of Mary, and the overall religious contempt for English Protestantism were all strong motivators for Philip II to prepare an invasion of England. In the mid-1580s, England had graduated from clandestine support for the Protestants in the Netherlands to full-blown military intervention. The troops being sent there and the incessant privateer raids wreaked havoc on Spanish trade in the area, on top of chipping away at the prestige of the dominant naval superpower of that time.

Francis Drake's 1587 attack on the Spanish naval base in Cádiz was the final straw. In the devastating attack, the privateers plundered anything they could and torched dozens of ships right in the middle of Spanish home waters. After this outrage, Philip began assembling the mighty Spanish Armada. Spain commanded a much vaster colonial empire at the time, but the gap between English and Spanish naval power in the waters of Europe was slowly narrowing in the late 1580s. The Royal Navy's home fleet enjoyed numerical superiority, but Spanish galleons were more formidable and possessed greater firepower.

The Spanish Armada is a historical name given to the fleet that Philip II of Spain assembled specifically to invade England in the summer of 1588. This task force numbered more than 130 ships and was hailed as invincible. Sure of his inevitable victory, Philip sent the fleet from Lisbon to the Netherlands to link up with reinforcements and then proceed towards England. While deceptively weaker on paper, the English fleet matched the Armada in numbers, but it did so with smaller, more maneuverable ships. The English also commanded a core of 20 of their own galleons, which made up in firepower what they lacked in numbers.

Stormy weather, the nimbleness of English ships, and superior tactics eventually led England to victory – which was a severe blow to Spain's naval prestige. Ever the proactive monarch, Elizabeth I, clad in armor and atop a horse, met her armies at Tilbury as they assembled for a potential battle in defense of London. As the naval battle unfolded, Elizabeth spoke before her troops, stressing that a woman's physical weakness should not obscure the "heart and stomach of a king" that she possessed.

Around 100 English troops died in the naval engagements. The Spanish Armada barely escaped with half its fleet, relentlessly attacked as it retreated all the way around Scotland, leaving behind up to 15,000 dead. This staggering triumph was the great payoff from all the investments that the House of Tudor had allocated to the Royal Navy, and it marked the irrefutable assertion of England as one of the great naval powers of the day.

Chapter 4: Shakespeare and Marlowe: Shaping the English Language

Cultural achievements of England and Britain entered the annals of history and school curricula throughout the world a long time ago. Due to the flourishing environment of art, creativity, and culture under Elizabeth I, the world has been embellished with such great creative minds as William Shakespeare and Christopher Marlowe. Although they were far from the only playwrights and wordsmiths of the Elizabethan era, these two creative geniuses were the embodiment of how English culture and language developed by leaps and bounds

Christopher Marlowe. [10]

in the 16th century. They also represent the linguistic consolidation and resulting philosophical development of their country, which is a decisive turning point in any nation's maturation and progress.

William Shakespeare

William Shakespeare is synonymous with England in literature and theater, but this preeminence reaches far beyond his homeland. Subjective tastes can differ, but impact and legacy can almost be measured, and those of Shakespeare have defined him as the most legendary dramatist in the world. There is hardly a language into which his plays have not been translated, and these immortal works continue to dominate theaters in every corner of the globe to this day.

Cataloging all the playwrights, writers, and various other artists that Shakespeare's work has influenced since the 16th century would be a herculean task. Competition is stiff, but it is relatively easy to make the case that no writer in the English language has influenced the world as much as William Shakespeare.

Early Life and the Lost Years

There is a moderate amount of mystery surrounding Shakespeare's private life, but not for a lack of contemporary references and facts about the man. This is perhaps the reason why he has been subject to quite a bit of speculation over the centuries regarding everything from his appearance to sexual orientation and personal beliefs. On the wilder side of that speculation is the matter of authorship of Shakespeare's work, with a handful of researchers suggesting that some of the work attributed to him might have been written by other authors. However, these theories only began to emerge more than two centuries after Shakespeare died. Although they persist to this day, the theories are widely considered to be fringe and are advocated by very few academics.

Theories aside, William Shakespeare was born in a market town called Stratford-upon-Avon, located around 100 miles northwest of London. His exact date of birth hasn't been confirmed but is estimated to have been April 23, 1564, with his baptism carried out three days later on April 26. William's father, John, was a busy man, trying his hand at all sorts of businesses, including farming, leatherwork, wood trade, and even money lending, among other ventures. He also got involved with the local administration, spending some time in a number of municipal offices. His wife, Mary Arden, came from money as she was born to a wealthy landowner. Not much else is known about William Shakespeare's parents, but there are indications that they might have been Catholics during the Reformation. They had a total of eight children, William being the third among them. Three of his siblings died at a very young age.

There is also a degree of disagreement regarding Shakespeare's early education, but given that his parents were fairly well-off, he probably went to a decent secondary school close to where he grew up. At this point in his education, Shakespeare was likely introduced to Latin and had an opportunity to study classic literature, which may have planted the seeds of creativity in his mind. What became of his education is unknown, as he might have taken up an apprenticeship with his father during adolescence.

Shakespeare married Anne Hathaway when he was just 18, even though she was around eight years older. Seeing as Shakespeare's first daughter, Susanna, was born just several months after the wedding, it's speculated that he and Anne entered marriage after finding out that she was pregnant. Two years later, in 1585, Shakespeare and Anne had twins, Hamnet and Judith. Hamnet was Shakespeare's only son, and he tragically passed away at age 11. For much of the following years, Shakespeare was primarily absent from home, focusing on writing and theater in London.

Among the historiographers of Shakespeare, the period between 1585 and 1592 is known as his "lost years." This gap in information is somewhat peculiar because the way in which Shakespeare resurfaced in historical records in 1592 clearly indicates that he had become quite well-known around the theater scene in London. This first new mention comes from a pamphlet put together by Robert Greene, a playwright who didn't have many nice things to say about Shakespeare.

Labeling Shakespeare an "upstart crow beautified with our feathers," Greene's pamphlet implied that Shakespeare didn't belong among the higher theater class due to his lack of university credentials. He was essentially calling him a charlatan who couldn't hold a candle to the so-called University Wits, a group of distinguished Elizabethan playwrights that included Greene, Christopher Marlowe, and others.

There is no consensus on what Shakespeare might have been doing during his lost years, and the wide range of proposed theories offers strikingly different ideas. It has been suggested that he might have had to flee the country due to a poaching incident, studied law, taught at a school, traveled Europe, or taken up acting in Stratford. The only thing that is certain is that by 1592, Shakespeare had already taken decisive steps into acting and writing.

Shakespeare's Work and Influence

Most of Shakespeare's principal works were produced in the period roughly between 1589 and 1613. By 1592, Shakespeare had already dabbled into the three primary genres of drama: tragedy, comedy, and history. His work within the genre of tragedy during the early years is best exemplified by Titus Andronicus, written sometime between 1588 and 1593 and widely regarded as his first tragedy. Comedies include The Comedy of Errors and The Taming of the Shrew. Distinguished among his historical works are Richard III and Henry VI, the latter being a trilogy.

Many of Shakespeare's most legendary works, such as Hamlet, Macbeth, Othello, and Romeo and Juliet, were tragedies, but during his early playwriting, he was known more for his comedies and histories. As early as 1592, Shakespeare displayed an advanced knowledge and understanding of London's culture, geography, and political affairs. He held an equally impressive grasp on similar topics in other European countries, including the affairs of royalty both at home and abroad. Some interpret his versatile knowledge and awareness of worldly affairs as somewhat strange for someone who grew up in the countryside. This is probably the main reason behind some of the suspicions regarding the authorship of Shakespeare's work, which persist to this day.

William Shakespeare. [11]

Throughout the 1590s, Shakespeare continued writing prolifically while also acting in various theaters and actor groups. Particularly notable was his time with the Lord Chamberlain's Men acting company, which he joined in 1594. The troupe was later renamed King's Men after King James I became a patron. Shakespeare was their writer and essential partner, eventually working together to establish the famous Globe Theatre in the late 1590s.

By the time he retired and went on to live his final years with his wife around 1613, Shakespeare had authored more than 37 plays. Many of his plays, such as All's Well That Ends Well, Troilus and Cressida, and Measure for Measure, can be interpreted as tragicomedies. Their defiance of classification has led some Shakespearean scholars to label them as "problem plays." One of the defining characteristics of Shakespeare's writing style was that he often gave his characters certain self-addressing monologues, also known as soliloquies. Hamlet's question of whether to be or not to be, addressed to himself, is the most famous example. Shakespeare was an all-around outstanding wordsmith, and his writing often involved various elements of wordplay. His usual poetic form was blank verse and iambic pentameter.

Shakespeare was a student of classical theater, often taking inspiration from the stages of ancient Greece and putting his own modern spin on them. Arguably, Shakespeare is most celebrated for his tragedies, which is probably because they allowed his insights into human psychology and emotions to shine the brightest. The exploration of human nature through psychologically and emotionally complex characters, with a frequent focus on conflict, is a common theme in Shakespeare's works. Some of the stories are more clear-cut, while others present a roller coaster of emotion, tonal shifts, and moral conundrums. Dramatic shifts in that regard are especially apparent in the "problem plays" and are one of the main reasons why they've been difficult to classify. Shakespearean psychology has been widely studied, primarily through characters like Hamlet. Sigmund Freud, for instance, was fascinated and intrigued by Hamlet, who inspired a lot of his work in trying to understand human nature.

Shakespeare was also an avid and accomplished poet. In his poetry, Shakespeare explored themes such as eroticism, love, aesthetics, the concept of truth, and much more. Shakespeare's sonnet collection abounds in sexuality as well as dark emotional subjects, often interwoven. Very explicit for their time in the early 17th century, Shakespeare's sonnets might have been his private poetry, published without his knowledge or blessing. One of Shakespeare's notable narrative poems was Venus and Adonis, a rather erotic piece dedicated to his friend Henry Wriothesley. Also dedicated to Henry was The Rape of Lucrece. Shakespeare's decision to dedicate such sexually charged material to his male friend is one of the reasons why there has been speculation on his potential homosexuality.

Shakespeare's death is usually dated April 23, 1616, when he was 52. Almost five centuries after his birth, virtually every man, woman, and child in the world has heard the name of Shakespeare. Not only did he inspire countless writers and artists of all vocations to this day, but he was instrumental in setting the stage for modern drama and theater. Shakespeare's linguistic legacy is also immense, and it's likely that no other writer has affected the English language to such an extent. A number of words were either created or popularized by Shakespeare, but his works also left behind various expressions. "Foregone conclusion," "wild goose chase," and "in a pickle" are only some of the examples that can be traced to Othello, Romeo and Juliet, and The Tempest, respectively.

Christopher Marlowe

Those who hold Shakespeare to be the most legendary playwright in history usually place Christopher Marlowe as a close second, at least among the playwrights of the Elizabethan era. Marlowe was a trailblazer in many regards, pioneering techniques like blank verse poetry. He was also highly regarded and belonged to the elite of the stage in London, a level of esteem that Shakespeare lacked in his early career.

According to a number of scholars, Marlowe had likely exerted significant influence on Shakespeare and his work. His plays were noted for their realistic displays of human emotion and infused with humanistic messages, yet they were often distinctly violent in language and the actions of his characters. Marlowe and Shakespeare were likely born within a couple of months of each other, which made for an exciting dynamic of mutual influence in an era of blooming artistic creation.

A Mysterious Youth

There is no clear record of Marlowe's birthday, but he was born in Canterbury in England's county of Kent. Records show that he was baptized on February 26, 1564. An unclear date of birth for someone living in the 16th century isn't all that mysterious, but some other aspects of Marlowe's early life definitely were. Marlowe died at age 29, attaining his great literary legacy in just a few short years of active work.

Early in his youth, Marlowe seemed to have been following a typical path befitting a talented young boy and diligent student. He attended The King's School on a scholarship and continued to perform well in his studies, which enabled him to enroll at Corpus Christi College in Cambridge in the 1580s. He graduated in 1584 with a bachelor's in arts and continued his education in the pursuit of a master's degree. He was set to get it in 1587, but then the university began holding up the process.

It isn't entirely clear what happened, but problems had likely emerged due to Marlowe's many supposed absences and rumors that he was looking to become a Catholic. This alleged plan of Marlowe's would have entailed his relocation to northern France, where he would attend an English seminary and eventually be ordained as a Catholic priest. At the time, this was a serious crime.

All these speculations were dispelled when the queen's Privy Council intervened by sending a letter on Marlowe's behalf. In the letter, they explained that Marlowe had done commendable service to the queen, working on "matters touching the benefit of his country." A direct intervention by such a high body of the monarchy on Marlowe's behalf was strange, to say the least, as was the cryptic description of his "services." As peculiar as the letter was, it definitely did the trick for Marlowe, and he was soon granted his master's.

The running theory among scholars is that Marlowe was employed as a secret agent or spy of some sort. The Privy Council's letter stressed that the queen was dissatisfied to see that an individual who had carried out such important service to the state was being "defamed by those ignorant of the affairs he went about." Whatever the truth of the matter was, Marlowe would resume his career path after being cleared, and he soon moved to London to begin his work as a writer from 1587 onward.

Brief Writing Career and a Strange, Untimely End

Among today's scholars, Marlowe is considered to have been the most distinguished dramatist in London during his short career. The trouble with his work is that a considerable portion of it has been poorly preserved and corrupted over the centuries. This is the unfortunate reality of his most famous play, The Tragical History of The Life and Death of Doctor Faustus. Scholars have also been struggling to establish a clear chronology of the works Marlowe published. He is considered a crucial predecessor to Shakespeare, having inspired some of his plays and charted a path for some of his genres. For instance, Marlowe's Edward the Second was an early example of a historical tragedy, a concept that Shakespeare would perfect with his famous histories. Edward the Second is also believed to be Marlowe's best-preserved piece, having suffered the most minor alteration from transcriptions and edits.

THE DEVIL AND Dᴿ FAUSTUS.

An illustration of Doctor Faustus, a play by Marlowe. [12]

Dido, Queen of Carthage, was likely Marlowe's first play, but it was only published in 1594, a year after his death. His second play, Tamburlaine the Great, was an important milestone in playwriting because it was one of the first blank-verse plays to be widely performed in London. The Jew of Malta and The Massacre at Paris are also essential parts of Marlowe's oeuvre. These two plays, along with Doctor Faustus and Edward the Second, are thought to be principally responsible for Marlowe's fame and subsequent legacy.

Marlowe's work explored many essential themes, and plays such as The Massacre at Paris were known for their graphic violence. Marlowe's plays widely present religious conflicts, vengeance, political schemes, corruption, and other mature themes. Doctor Faustus dramatized the old German legend of Faust, which is a story about a scholar who makes a pact with the Devil in pursuit of power and advanced knowledge. Marlowe's play puts a darker spin on the story by giving it a tragic ending in which the protagonist never repents in time and is eventually taken by demons.

At the time, the most celebrated London playwright met his end in 1593 under unclear circumstances that have sparked endless debate and theories. One theory is that he was killed for blasphemy or atheism, while another suggests it was merely a tragic outcome of a particularly ferocious bar fight. Others have theorized that he might have been a homosexual and attacked out of bigotry or passion. Betrayal and jealousy by another playwright have also been posited as potential answers.

Yet another and perhaps more attractive proposition is that Marlowe was killed amid the intrigues of the world of espionage. It certainly seems odd that records would be so slim and unreliable regarding the death of one of the most revered artists in London at the time. Coupled with the indications that Marlowe was indeed involved in the intelligence apparatus, the lack of documents describing his death might suggest a deliberate cover-up. Unfortunately, it's unlikely that explanations of Marlowe's death will ever move past conjecture.

While he might be considered number two among the Elizabethan dramatists from today's perspective, Marlowe was a legend in his day. Held in the utmost regard and deeply entrenched in the highest echelons of theater, he helped define the culture and arts of the Elizabethan era. It is difficult to say what could have become of Marlowe's legacy had his work been better preserved and had he lived past his twenties.

Chapter 5: Isaac Newton and Robert Hooke: Unraveling the Universe

One of the most critical ways in which England has left its mark upon the world is through science. English contributions in this field are numerous, involving natural sciences but also the many breakthroughs in technology and engineering that came a bit later. These groundbreaking discoveries occurred within the larger context of a period known in historiography as the Scientific Revolution, which took place between the 16th and 17th centuries.

One of the most essential stages in the development of humanity, this period saw a gradual but radical shift in the approach to understanding the world. The old ways of philosophy gave way to the scientific method, leading to a flourishing of knowledge and invention. New technologies and the increasing institutional support for further breakthroughs carried the process. Over time, a growing number of countries would establish institutions designed explicitly for scientific pursuits. This ensured resources and conditions for individual scientists to conduct their historic work like never before.

Galileo Galilei. [13]

This 200-year period witnessed many magnificent minds, such as Galileo Galilei, Andreas Versalius, and countless others. The Scientific Revolution initially blossomed in Europe, eventually spreading across the world. England was home to many scientific pioneers at that time, including the famed Isaac Newton and Robert Hooke. The story of these two great minds is one of progress and intellectual pursuit on an unprecedented scale. However, it is also a tale of grudges, pride, and competition that is all too human.

Isaac Newton

The developments of the Scientific Revolution should never be narrowed down to one single person, but it's not too out of line to say that Isaac Newton's name is all but synonymous with it. He wasn't the first to devote his life to scientific discovery, but his incredible breakthroughs in mathematics and especially physics represent a culmination of the entire period.

Newton's name, through the natural laws he identified, lives on in schools in all corners of the globe to this day, and it will likely remain there forever. The human understanding of gravity and motion – both critical aspects of the way reality on this planet is experienced – can be traced back directly to Newton's work. Through his contributions, he has etched his name in history in a way that only the most glorified artists, conquerors, and religious leaders could boast.

Personal Life and Philosophy of Knowledge

Much has been said about some of the more glaring difficulties in Isaac Newton's character, particularly his temperamental nature and propensity to take things to heart. Newton's early life, both in childhood and later youth, was marked by a number of setbacks, most of which were entirely out of his control. Isaac was born on December 25, 1642, Old Style (4 January 1643 on the Gregorian calendar, which is now used) in the village of Woolsthorpe-by-Colsterworth in eastern England. His folks were a yeoman family of farmers, the closest thing that 17th-century England had to a middle class. Isaac never met his father, as he had died some months before his birth. His mother, Hannah Ayscough, was later remarried to a minister.

In his childhood, Isaac spent some years away from his mother at the request of his stepfather, who died when Isaac was 14. There has been some speculation that these years of separation from parental love might have profoundly impacted Isaac's development, leading to problems with his temper and social interaction later in life. From a young age, Isaac kept his mind occupied with anything that had to do with mechanics, often tinkering with various models and small inventions. It was clear that he was a gifted boy, but he seemed more interested in focusing on his personal projects than school, where he often under-performed.

Isaac's inventive mind would sometimes bring him to mischief and get him in trouble. In one recorded incident, he instigated a public panic in his village by launching lit lanterns into the sky at night. Some of the locals interpreted the lights as a meteor shower, causing fear and frustration in the village. Still, none of Isaac's occasional mischief caused any real problems, and people around him tended to notice and appreciate the keenness of his mind. He didn't get the most appropriate guidance, however, as he was initially expected to study law at Trinity College in Cambridge. He began his academic pursuits in 1661, but it quickly became clear that his mind longed for mathematics.

One of the essential teachers on Isaac's early path was Isaac Barrow, with whom Newton attended private lessons in mathematics. Isaac Newton took private classes because he felt his regular education wasn't providing all the knowledge he needed. This was the beginning of an important relationship, as Barrow would become instrumental in propelling Newton's academic career later on. After graduation in 1665, this career would encounter a significant obstacle in the form of a Black Death outbreak in one of the disease's many recurrences after the Middle Ages. As many public institutions closed down for the duration, Isaac had to go back home and put his career on hold for about a year.

This break he had to take did little to subdue Isaac's thirst for scientific pursuits. Between 1665 and 1666, he undertook extensive research on his own, resulting in many important discoveries. Isaac himself was very pleased with his progress in a number of experiments during that time. The binomial theory, refraction of light, and other important studies of Isaac's all happened during that year. He also laid the groundwork for his research into the theory of universal gravitation, which would later become one of his most famous contributions to science.

In the pursuits of his mind, Isaac Newton didn't shy away from all sorts of approaches, some of which were radically different from each other. He experimented with a wide range of methods and philosophies, including mechanical philosophy and even alchemy. Newton delved deep into the past, thoroughly exploring ancient understandings of the world and saving the most important tidbits for later use in his experiments. He considered the sum of ancient and contemporary human knowledge to be of utmost importance.

Isaac Newton was an adherent of the idea that the job of modern science wasn't just to uncover new knowledge but also to rediscover truths that had long been understood and then lost over the millennia. Ever humbled by the great minds of the past, Newton saw himself as "standing on the shoulders of giants," as he once put it. He was also a Protestant and a believer in God as the prime mover who occasionally intervened to address the physical imperfections of the world, which Newton discovered in his work. Isaac Newton was also a very private person who preferred to conduct much of his work in secrecy, although he eventually published his monumental findings.

Sir Isaac Newton. [14]

Discoveries and an Immortal Legacy

One of the fields where Newton's work charted new paths was optics and the wider study of light. Although his initial discoveries were significant, he had trouble getting his ideas to gain traction in the mainstream, particularly in the Royal Society of London for Improving Natural Knowledge. He needed something tangible and comprehensive to attract interest and lend weight to his research, and so he designed and constructed the first reflective telescope. Newton's revolutionary telescope was completed in 1668, instantly garnering praise and getting him accepted into the Royal Society four years later. His telescope was ten times smaller than previous designs, clearer, and had a 40x time magnification.

The research that led to Newton's telescope focused on much more than creating a viable product, though. Newton was essentially the man who discovered that white light is the sum of a spectrum of natural colors, which he figured out through his experiments with prisms, refraction, and projection. He also used multiple prisms to split light into the differently colored parts and direct the separate rays elsewhere, realizing that they remained in their respective colors after the second prism.

It thus became clear that light is heterogeneous, which revolutionized the way it was perceived and understood. This new theory went contrary to conventional understanding and was met with some backlash, notably from Robert Hooke. Hooke dismissed Newton's findings and even leveled baseless accusations of plagiarism, leading to a complete falling out between the two distinguished scientists. Isaac Newton took umbrage and left the Royal Society soon thereafter in protest, refusing to stay even when he was offered the presidency. He only considered returning after Robert Hooke died in 1703. The following year, Newton published all of his work in optics, which eventually entered the very core of what the study of optics is nowadays.

In the wider public, Isaac Newton is more famous for his work regarding the theory of gravity and his study of motion. Contrary to popular mythology, Isaac Newton didn't suddenly understand that gravity existed because an apple fell on his head. However, observing the falling of fruits likely inspired him to delve deeper into the subject. The existence and effects of gravity have been well-established since ancient times, with various theories proposed. Back when people thought that the Earth was the center of the universe, a widespread theory of gravity was that there was an inexplicable force within the planet's core, pulling all of reality toward it.

As usual, Newton's research was inspired by ancient natural philosophy, such as the work of Claudius Ptolemy, who presented his view of planetary astronomy in the 2nd century. What Claudius and more recent researchers like Nicolaus Copernicus had in common is that they thought planets moved along a perfectly circular path around the Sun. It wasn't until the time of German astronomer Johannes Kepler (1571-1630) that it became understood that heavenly bodies followed an elliptical path. This discovery was based on the observation that planets would speed up as they got closer to the Sun.

It was Newton's subsequent study of gravity that finally explained this phenomenon. Newton presented his groundbreaking theory of gravity in

1687 with the Mathematical Principles of Natural Philosophy, commonly known and shortened as Principia Mathematica. This monumental work brought together mathematics and mechanics, explaining the theory of gravity after elaborating on what became known as Newton's laws of motion. The three laws outlined are now taught to children in schools across the planet. Principia Mathematica then went on to describe gravity as an attraction force between any two bodies in the universe, primarily dependent on their mass and distance.

It was a theory with universal applications, explaining everything from a planet's revolution around its star to why an apple falls to the ground. The only problem was that nobody could understand why this mysterious force existed and where it originated from – it simply was. This perplexed many scientists, philosophers, theologians, and anyone else who studied Newton's work. Those who believed in God as the true mover of all things in the universe generally had an easier time coming to grips with Newton's new science.

Unlike some other great minds of history, Newton lived to see the recognition and fruits of his work. He enjoyed a rather productive and successful academic career and even dabbled in politics. His international recognition landed him a spot in the French Royal Academy of Sciences in 1699. After the death of Hooke and his appointment as the president of the Royal Society, Newton exerted significant influence to popularize a more practical approach to science, encouraging experiments. He also played a prominent role in Britain's Royal Mint, which contributed to his subsequent knighting by Queen Anne in 1705.

His personal life, and especially his relationships with other scientists, stayed tumultuous, including conflicts such as the one with German mathematician Leibniz. Unwed and childless, Newton lived a quiet, solitary life in his later years, focusing on studying the Bible. He passed away on March 20, 1727. As famous and celebrated as he was in life, it was in the centuries following his death that the true weight of his legacy became clear, thanks to all the new scientific breakthroughs that depended so heavily on the path he had charted. The 20th-century relativity and quantum physics discoveries were the first time anybody would move physics as far forward as Newton did.

Robert Hooke

Robert Hooke's story was one of genius but also struggle. Widely regarded as another essential contributor during the Scientific Revolution, he helped the scientific development of mankind whilst also, by the characteristics of his path, highlighting the socioeconomic injustices of the day. Through talent, hard work, and resourcefulness, Hooke would leave behind an eternal legacy despite the odds that were often stacked against him.

Early Life and Contributions

Robert was born into poverty on July 18, 1635. The academic opportunities available to him were very limited, just as some of his later endeavors would be hindered by this unenviable position. As far as Robert Hooke was concerned, however, this only meant he had to work harder, and that he did.

Through sheer talent and commitment, he was able to enroll in Oxford University, where he was lucky enough to find appreciation for his gifted nature. Reputed anatomist Robert Boyle and physician Thomas Willis took the young student under their wing and brought him on as a lab assistant. Boyle quickly became Hooke's mentor, and the two scientists formed a lasting, fruitful relationship.

Robert Hooke. [15]

However, Robert struggled to make ends meet without a notable product or idea to sell, but it wasn't long until he solved this problem, too. He was able to get a job as an architect and surveyor in London, which netted a substantial salary. Fate extended her hand to Robert as well; London had gone through the Great Fire in 1666, leaving huge amounts of work for people like him. He was able to amass a considerable sum of money and buy his freedom from work, providing time and resources he could devote to science. Throughout his work during London's great reconstruction, Hooke extensively collaborated with Christopher Wren.

Robert Hooke's relationship with the Royal Society had a rocky start, likely in part due to the unfortunate circumstances of his birth. He wasn't taken on as a founder, and it took some time and some string-pulling by Boyle to get Robert instated at a lower position. Even then, it seemed as though the Royal Society would always drag its feet whenever Hooke was due a promotion or recognition. In fairness, Hooke's way up the academic ladder might have also been partly held back by his lack of accomplishments in mathematics at that time. His contributions, especially in anything that had to do with experimentation, however, were hard to ignore.

A Hidden World Beyond the Human Eye

Hooke was particularly interested in technological progress, attributing great importance to the development of new, more capable instruments. He felt that leaps in technology would be the key to propel science forward, so he focused on everything that had to do with mechanics and engineering. This was reflected in his many experiments at the Royal Society, which revolved around equipment and instruments of all sorts. Navigation instruments, optics, and clocks were some of the areas of his most notable achievements.

Unlike Boyle, Newton, and many other great minds of England during that time, Robert Hooke was a mechanic and engineer through and through. His work took little inspiration from theological pursuits and didn't focus too much on theoretical research, opting instead for real, practical inventions above all else. It is not that Hooke was an opponent of religion, though, as he was certainly well-liked in the Church and even by the Archbishop of Canterbury. Despite the many obstacles Hooke had to overcome in his life, the only truly ugly episode of his career was the spat with Isaac Newton.

The greatest issue with this conflict was that it was very public. Since Hooke and Newton were considered two of the greatest minds at that time, they both had many admirers and allies. As the controversy intensified, many people within academic circles and beyond began to take sides and get involved. This led to fractures and all manner of unpleasantness in the scientific community, likely wasting a lot of valuable time and potential collaborations in the process.

One of Hooke's greatest strides into widespread fame was his contribution to microscopy. He created a sensation when he published Micrographia in 1665. Robert Hooke wasn't the inventor of the microscope, but he substantially improved it and made better use of it than anyone before him. Microscopes at that time were notoriously sensitive and difficult to operate, causing most users to end up with a blurry image of the object. Thanks to his technical improvements and incredible instrument skills, Hooke got perfectly clear images of insects and various everyday objects. He then drew what he saw in great detail and had the drawings engraved, collecting all of these images and his detailed microscope manual into Micrographia.

The book was a hit with the wider public and scientists alike, showing well-known objects in a way nobody could have imagined before. The effect of these pictures was so profound that the book even sparked religious discussions and debates about intelligent design. People were shocked that a simple housefly was such a complex, fascinating organism. This widespread fascination was also a huge boost for microscope manufacturers, as everyone wanted one. Unfortunately, even with Hooke's improvements and published instructions, most people still struggled to get such clear images, so the sensation waned over time.

Hooke also dabbled in theoretical work, making contributions to the understanding of Jupiter's astronomy, fossils, and, notably, springs. Hooke's Law is the result of his work in this area, making it possible to measure the pressure and elasticity of springs. Still, Hooke was, first and foremost, a hands-on scientist obsessed with practical experiments, and his own body wouldn't be spared from this obsession. He was known to experiment extensively on himself, ingesting dubious medicines, poisonous plants, chemicals, drugs like opium, and metals, which he added to his wine. Despite all this, he lived to be 67 years old, dying on March 3, 1703. Hooke is remembered for his versatility as a scientist and as the man who pioneered the perfection of instruments and equipment with a focus on accuracy, rightly believing this to be one of the cornerstones of future scientific progress.

Chapter 6: John Locke and William Wilberforce: Philosophies of Freedom

As England gradually waltzed into its era of true power at an international level, it had already achieved great strides in law, military strength, literature, and science. With such strong foundations, the nation could pursue prosperity on a whole new level. This allowed optimal conditions for philosophy to develop in the early modern era in England and across Europe, where numerous other nations followed a similar developmental trajectory.

In the Salon of Madame Geoffrin, a painting by Charles Lemonnier that represents the Age of Enlightenment. [16]

One of the consequences was the Age of Enlightenment in the 17th and 18th centuries, in which John Locke played an important early role. This era of rationalism would revolutionize virtually every level of English and European society, with enormous historical implications. In one way or another, it led to the refinement of ideas about liberty, rights, constitutional government, secularism, and much more. The era also had a notable effect on morality, casting a new light on some of the practices once considered acceptable. The abolition of the slave trade, relentlessly pursued by William Wilberforce, illustrates how some of the Enlightenment ideas eventually culminated and were put into practice.

John Locke

Apart from his philosophical contributions, John Locke was also a physicist. As one of the greatest English minds of the Enlightenment, he pioneered empiricism in Britain and left a tremendous mark on political philosophy, especially regarding government, the social contract, and personal liberty. Some of the greatest philosophical minds widely explored in basic sociology classes, such as Voltaire and Jean-Jacques Rousseau, were considerably influenced by Locke.

Personal liberty, rights, limits on government power and size, rule of law, and representation in government were all key aspects of Locke's political philosophy. The influence of all these ideas is strikingly apparent throughout political life and discourse in the West today, more than 300 years after Locke's death. Locke's philosophy quickly penetrated into sociopolitical spaces well beyond Britain, making its way into the ideology behind the American Revolution and the Declaration of Independence. For his contributions to early liberal theory, John Locke is often regarded as the "father of liberalism."

Life, Academia, and Politics

Locke was born on August 29, 1632, in the village of Wrington, Somerset, in the southwest of England. His life path might have been inspired by his father, also John, who worked as a lawyer and a clerk. Locke's father also participated in the English Civil War in the mid-17th century, fighting on the side of the Parliamentarians. Whether his father's legacy had planted the seeds of Locke's later views on government cannot be known for certain, but that legacy and its perks helped get young John enrolled at the prestigious Westminster School.

John Locke would come to be a highly educated man, spending the period between 1652 and 1667 committed to his studies. He subsequently gave lectures in metaphysics, logic, and other subjects at Christ Church at the University of Oxford. On top of that, Locke studied medicine and would make a close acquaintance with a number of distinguished scientists and academics at Oxford. Another important acquaintance who would play a significant role in Locke's life was Anthony Ashley Cooper, who was a member of Parliament, with whom he formed a friendship.

Cooper would eventually become the Earl of Shaftesbury while maintaining his close friendship with Locke. By then, a learned man of medicine, Locke was employed as the earl's home physician and would even perform a difficult surgery on him at one point. Locke and the earl stayed close for a long time, with Locke partaking in his friend's fate even when he got embroiled in political troubles.

Things got especially heated in the late 1670s when the Earl of Shaftesbury tried to exclude James, the Catholic Duke of York, from royal succession. When the duke was crowned James II, despite the efforts of the earl and his allies, Cooper had to flee the country. Locke followed him into exile shortly after his friend left for Holland in 1682. Locke finally returned to England after James II was deposed in the Glorious Revolution of 1688, restoring Protestant rule with William III.

Over the many years that Locke spent under the patronage of Shaftesbury, he devoted himself to writing and developing his political philosophy. Locke's distinguished patron exerted significant influence on his philosophy. Just as he followed Shaftesbury in the eventual political fallout, Locke also followed him during the earlier, more peaceful part of his political career. 1672 was when Locke's political involvements began in earnest, so he would spend quite a few years in service to Shaftesbury before publishing his first works.

A notable aspect of the Earl of Shaftesbury's political career was his founding and leadership of the Whig movement, a party strongly opposed to the Tories. The staple of Whig politics was the advocacy of constitutional monarchism, with a nuanced view on how the monarchy should function, what the government should and should not do, and, most importantly, the government's relationship with the governed. During these active political years of his life, John Locke absorbed and eventually molded many of his key political views. All the while, he wrote.

Father of Liberalism

After he returned to England, Locke had a very active six-year period in which he published his most essential writings, exposing the world to his philosophies. Lots of this work had been put together quite a while before publishing, but it had to be kept private. Indeed, some of John Locke's most essential works, such as the Two Treatises of Government, were published anonymously to avoid political repercussions and persecution.

As a staunch empiricist, Locke argued that human knowledge could only be acquired through the gathering and analysis of facts, which, in turn, could only be acquired through sensory experiences. This view opposes the idea that knowledge, or at least some forms, could be innate or attained from something beyond the individual experiencing the world through the senses. As a man committed to science, Locke believed that knowledge could also be sought in places that lay beyond the individual's basic perception of the world. To that end, he advocated the scientific method with a particular emphasis on thorough experimentation.

Locke delved into this theory in his Essay Concerning Human Understanding, published in 1689 and written during his time in the Netherlands. Also, during that time, he wrote the Letter on Toleration. These ideas were a major factor influencing the thinking of many distinguished minds of the Enlightenment. His advocacy of scientific experimentation ensured that Locke's influence reached well beyond political philosophy and was instrumental in shaping the Scientific Revolution.

In The Two Treatises of Government, published in 1690, Locke outlined some of his most important political and philosophical views. The views he expressed could be interpreted as defining the founding principles of democracy as it is understood today. One of the most radical views that this publication expressed was that monarchs did not have a divine right to rule. This was an attack on one of the core tenets of governance both in England and overseas, which had been widely accepted throughout medieval Europe.

John Locke. [17]

Locke believed instead that societies should be governed based on mutual agreements between the government and the governed. In practice, this meant that kings could and should be replaced if disapproved of by their subjects. This view was one of the fundamental principles in the philosophy of Thomas Jefferson and the American Declaration of Independence in 1776. Locke defined every man's three essential natural rights: life, liberty, and property, which are now some of the pillars of the concept of universal human rights.

One of the particularly fascinating aspects of Locke's legacy is his view on property, which he defined as the product of one's labor. This idea greatly influenced both Adam Smith and Karl Marx, who are considered two of the greatest economic minds in history and the progenitors of two famously antithetical ideologies or economic models. The capitalist and communist viewpoints continue vying for primacy to this very day. John

Locke's other important views were outlined in the Thoughts Concerning Education and a series called Letters Concerning Toleration. These writings advocated an improved status for students and freedom of religion, albeit with exceptions regarding atheism and Catholicism due to the specifics of English politics and conflicts at that time.

John Locke was one of those thinkers who were so far ahead of their time that the residue of their philosophy permeates today's world with incredible clarity. His high regard for individualism, property rights, and personal liberty is easily identifiable as the foundation of liberalism. It is also strikingly apparent in the political culture, discourse, and systems in the US, Western Europe, the wider Anglosphere, and international conventions. John Locke died on October 28, 1704, aged 72. He spent his final moments in the company of a fellow philosopher and dear friend, Damaris Cudworth.

William Wilberforce

In his day, William Wilberforce was an accomplished politician and British MP. In parliament, he represented Yorkshire as an independent member. However, William's life took a dramatic turn at one point in his career, and he began to change his entire outlook. He gradually became obsessed with all manner of reform, which led him toward his most important legacy: the abolition of Britain's participation in the slave trade.

In fact, Wilberforce became so committed to reform and started to think so progressively that he even began championing animal rights, a very unusual pursuit during those times. Wilberforce was also somewhat of an anomaly as he was essentially conservative. His conservatism was mostly reflected in the domestic policies that he supported in England, which some had criticized as socially repressive while championing progressive causes abroad.

Personal Life, Politics, and Faith

On August 24, 1759, William Wilberforce was born in Kingston upon Hull, Yorkshire. He was born to privilege and wealth, the only son of Elizabeth Bird and Robert Wilberforce, a successful man involved in trade. It was William's grandfather who made the family fortune by trading in the Baltic Sea, but his father continued in the same vein. William relocated to London when he was still young, living with nonconformist Puritan relatives. He felt at home here, and the convictions of his relatives seemed to agree with him from a young age. However,

William's mother didn't like this, and he was eventually brought back to Hull, where he would be raised within the confines of Anglicanism.

His family made sure that he would receive a proper education, and he was enrolled in St John's College at Cambridge in 1776 when he was around 17. William had every temptation and opportunity to live a frivolous and carefree life as a young man. Just two years before he went to Cambridge, he came into a considerable inheritance after the death of his grandfather. He received yet another inheritance when his uncle died in 1777. William was not even out of his teens before he became financially independent.

His previously fervent religious adherence began to wane, and he started focusing more on socializing at Cambridge, so he did enjoy himself to an extent. However, he never developed a taste for drinking and other frivolities in which his colleagues routinely partook. Despite his aversion to such excesses, William was far from withdrawn and was never an outsider in the social life of his university. He didn't perform particularly well in his studies, but he made the most of his gift for conversation and communication. During his years at Cambridge, he met his friend, long-time ally, and future prime minister, William Pitt the Younger.

Toward the end of his time at Cambridge, Wilberforce decided to run for office, spending a hefty sum on his campaign to acquire a seat in parliament as a representative of his hometown of Hull. This was William's first entry into politics, an impressive feat for a 21-year-old who was still in college. He spent about four years in parliament before his life took a new, spiritual turn. While touring Europe with his family, Wilberforce stumbled upon some evangelical writings and was particularly captivated by Philip Doddridge's The Rise and Progress of Religion in the Soul.

This book enormously influenced Wilberforce's mind and spirituality, motivating him to come back to religion in a big way. He suddenly found himself introducing radical changes to his habits, lifestyle, and thinking. No longer content to be another rich kid merrily strolling through life without a care in the world, William started studying the Bible, ceased gambling, completely abandoned alcohol, and began rising early every day. William's path in life suddenly became clear to him as if through a divine revelation. He would stay on this path for the rest of his life, firmly committed to leaving the world in a better state than he had found it.

Ending an Era of Horrendous Exploitation

In his own words, his mission consisted of two great objectives set before him by God: to end the slave trade and reform morality. Wilberforce saw himself as a moral reformist in general, with abolition simply being the biggest and most important goal on that path. It took a while after his evangelical rebirth for William's main objective to be crystalized and realize that his purpose was to end slavery.

By the time Wilberforce joined the fight, the abolitionist movement was already at work. He came into contact with the cause around 1787 – after meeting Thomas Clarkson and a group of like-minded abolitionists gathered around him, who later became organized as the Testonites. The group saw Wilberforce as a suitable candidate to lobby for their goals in parliament. This was essentially a leadership role in the movement, which William found somewhat daunting. He strongly supported the cause but had doubts as to his ability to contribute in the way Clarkson and others wanted him to.

William Wilberforce. [18]

William ultimately accepted this historic mission, and by the late 1780s, he was already using his political position to further the cause. Thanks to the work of the Committee for the Abolition of the Slave Trade, the horrific iniquities of the slave trade were well-presented to the public by that time. The campaigners used testimonies from repentant participants in the slave trade, detailed posters presenting the appalling conditions on slave ships, and various other materials to effectively communicate their message. Christian sentiments regarding compassion, human dignity, and morality were particularly important in driving the campaign and turning the public against what was seen as one of Britain's greatest shames.

Political support for the cause grew in parliament, but the opponents of abolition had an enormous institution of a long-standing, well-established trade at their backs. The political process toward abolition would be a long, grueling endeavor. The first attempt to pass an abolitionist bill was presented in 1789, but a significant margin outvoted it. The abolitionists continued campaigning and trying to pass legislation, but circumstances such as Britain's conflict with France during the French Revolutionary Wars (1792-1802) forced abolition down the list of priorities.

The early 19th century saw a resurgence of interest in the topic. After Wilberforce's friend William Pitt died in 1806, the abolitionists gave it another try, this time using a strategy of incremental change. The proposed bill was limited, focusing primarily on forbidding slave merchants to trade with the colonies of France. The idea was to initially weaken the business while preparing a much more comprehensive abolition act for when the political climate improved. This approach was the brainchild of James Stephen, and it worked, probably owing to the general hostility felt toward France at that time. The slave trade persisted, but a huge portion of its revenue was eliminated.

After this crushing blow, an enormous breakthrough came sooner than expected. The following year saw the passing of the Slave Trade Act of 1807 by an overwhelming parliamentary majority. The trade of enslaved people was now officially illegal in the entirety of the British Empire. Unfortunately, this bill didn't free the enslaved people who had already been enslaved prior to the vote. From an economic standpoint, freeing all enslaved persons would have been a much greater upset than simply outlawing all future trade, so there was a lot more work to be done.

Wilberforce spent many subsequent years campaigning for the full abolition of the practice while also working on other matters. In this late phase of the movement, he found an important ally in Sir Thomas Fowell

Buxton around 1821. Together, they continued pushing for emancipation, leading to the establishment of the Anti-Slavery Society in 1823. Shortly thereafter, Wilberforce relinquished his parliamentary role to Buxton, effectively leaving him in charge of the political struggle. From 1825 onward, William spent his final years in retirement, still tuned into the news regarding his life's work. The Slavery Abolition Act passed a vote on July 26, 1833, and William Wilberforce died three days later at the age of 73.

Chapter 7: James Watt and George Stephenson: Steam and Steel

The Industrial Revolution was another decisive era that marked a turning point in human development. It was a period that fundamentally changed how many people lived and led to an unprecedented increase in urbanization. It was also a harsh time in many ways, as new means of production and a rapidly changing technological landscape collided with outdated legislation that struggled to keep up. Environmental issues, rough working conditions, child labor, the obsolescence of certain jobs due to machinery, and the emergence of capital as the main source of wealth and power instead of land ownership were only some of the hot topics of the day.

Iron and Coal, a painting by William Bell Scott that represents the Industrial Revolution.[19]

Of course, there are those who argue that progress inevitably comes at a cost, and the Industrial Revolution certainly saw no shortage of progress. Much of what keeps the manufacturing process and the global economy churning in today's times can be traced back directly to the Industrial Revolution. This time of great invention has been defined in a couple of different periods, with the widest and most accepted time frame being between 1760 and 1840. Great Britain was the epicenter from which the revolution's many breakthroughs originated and spread throughout the globe. Many great minds made their contribution to this era, with names such as James Watt and George Stephenson becoming synonymous with the period.

James Watt

As a Scottish inventor, James Watt is a reminder that English history is part of a greater British whole in which many invaluable contributions were made by people who didn't come from a pure English background. Watt was undoubtedly one of the most crucial figures in the overall development of mankind, leaving behind a legacy that directly shapes the world of today in ways that very few people have done. His epoch-defining work also illustrates that progress comes from a long chain of great thinkers whose genius draws from those before and conditions those who come after. James Watt didn't invent the steam engine, but he made sure that humanity could unlock the true potential of this world-altering invention.

Watt's Early Struggles

James Watt was born in the Scottish town of Greenock, Renfrewshire, on January 19, 1736. As a young boy, Watt was rather frail and prone to health issues, which resulted in him leading a somewhat sheltered life in his formative years. As a result, he received much of his early education by being home-schooled by his mother. From an early age, he expressed an interest in engineering and mechanics, especially accurate mathematical instruments such as scales, compasses, quadrants, and similar contraptions. Fortunately for James, from an early age, he had an opportunity to tinker with such instruments thanks to his father, who was a successful contractor involved in shipbuilding. James Watt Sr. ran several workshops as part of his business, allowing his son to come in and use various tools, benches, and anything else he needed to pursue his creative urges.

After spending a number of early years being home-schooled, James started to attend grammar school, where he took lessons in Greek, Latin, and mathematics. He didn't express much interest in the languages, but mathematics seemed to agree with him. Between his practical self-education in his father's workshops and the knowledge he was accumulating at school, James Watt would form a solid intellectual base for further learning by the time he was a teenager. By the age of 17, James knew what he wanted to do with his life: design and build instruments.

James Watt's first move in pursuit of a career came when he relocated to Glasgow in search of work. This was partly due to the fact that his father had begun experiencing troubles in his business endeavors, leading James to attempt to make money from his passion for making mathematical instruments. His initial stay in Glasgow was short-lived, as he soon moved on to London, where he sought additional training in his trade. It was around this time, when James was 18 years old, that his mother passed away, and his father's health began to deteriorate. James himself continued to struggle with his own health problems that had plagued him since childhood, and he suffered regular headaches.

The year he spent in London between 1755 and 1756 wasn't an easy time for Watt, but he managed to accumulate significant knowledge and skills thanks to his training in the capital. He returned to Glasgow in 1757 and decided to set up a shop where he would make and sell instruments. He encountered many obstacles in this undertaking, however, mainly due to his lack of experience, credentials, and connections.

It was then that fate finally decided to extend her hand to James Watt when he was given the opportunity to restore and improve astronomical instruments recently procured by the University of Glasgow. Watt's work was impressive and quickly garnered the attention of professors at the university. As a result, Watt was encouraged to open his workshop adjacent to the university. This was how he made the acquaintance of scientist Joseph Black and the legendary economist Adam Smith.

Unlocking the Power of Steam

James Watt first began looking into steam engines in 1759 when an acquaintance of his from the university, John Robinson, introduced him to the Newcomen engine. Newcomen's were very rudimentary designs that had already become quite obsolete by that time. These simple steam engines had been in use for almost five decades, mainly in mines as a way of pumping out water. Named after the man who invented and patented them in 1703, Thomas Newcomen, these early steam engines attracted John Robinson's attention as a potential way of powering motion. This was a rather novel idea at the time because the technological limitations of Newcomen engines didn't allow for such applications, but the principle was there, and Watt was hooked on the idea.

Early on, James Watt focused on just experimenting with steam power and trying to construct his own engine models. The experiments revolved around attaching steam cylinders and pistons to wheels connected by gears. The idea was to make a working model and try to use it to propel motion, as opposed to traditional Newcomen engines that were relegated to stationary roles. Watt's attempts to build a working model weren't successful, but the whole process helped him learn a lot about steam engines and thermal energy.

In late 1763 and early 1764, Watt was able to get his hands on a full-size Newcomen engine when another friend from the university invited him to fix one. Now that he was finally working with a steam engine, the thing that stuck out to Watt was how much steam was being wasted by the machine. This was precious energy that could have been directed to something useful, but instead, around three-quarters of the steam's thermal energy went to keeping the engine cylinder heated after each cycle.

James Watt. [20]

The engine would eventually introduce cold water into the cylinder to condense steam to bring down the pressure. This repeated heating and cooling process was the main problem, causing valuable thermal energy to go to waste and severely limiting the engine's usefulness for more complex tasks. What James Watt had to do was find a way to preserve all this heat and convert it into mechanical energy. In short, the biggest problem plaguing the existing steam engines of the day was inefficiency and terrible fuel economy.

In 1765, James Watt realized that the key to preserving a steam engine's latent heat was to separate the condensation process from the cylinder. He came up with the idea of creating a special chamber designated for condensation and connected to the cylinder. His solution became known as the separate condenser, his first major invention that changed everything. This revolutionary road wasn't easy, though. Watt had to struggle to get his invention patented, and further work to design and build a fully-fledged working engine required financing.

Watt's friend Joseph Black helped with a loan, which enabled Watt to build a simple but demonstrative test engine. Around this time, Watt also met and struck up a partnership with John Roebuck, a renowned scientist and inventor who had founded Carron Iron Works. After partnering up in 1768, Watt could do much more work on his design, and by the following year, he was able to secure a patent. Further difficulties arose when Roebuck went bankrupt in 1772, but Watt was able to overcome this hurdle by taking on Matthew Boulton as a partner. Boulton was a distinguished early industrialist who owned the Soho Manufactory factory close to Birmingham and could allocate significant resources to Watt's promising work. This lucrative partnership also ensured that Watt could extend his patent in 1775, pushing it to 1800. For the next 25 years, Boulton and Watt maintained their partnership, allowing the promising inventor access to well-trained workers and all the tools he needed. The perfection of the new steam engine could thus proceed at a much faster pace.

Throughout these years, Boulton was much more than a financier. He offered valuable guidance, solid business advice, and numerous clever ideas on how to continue improving the engine. Watt went on to secure numerous new patents by the time he would finalize his machine. The final touch came in 1790 with the introduction of the pressure gauge, at which point the Watt engine was nearly perfected. Watt lived to reap the benefits of his work, amassing considerable wealth before the final version of the engine was even done. Between Boulton's help and the steady trickle of royalties from his patents, Watt secured himself financially and could pursue various other endeavors. Both he and Boulton were admitted into the Royal Society in 1785.

Watt's engine quickly proliferated across several industries, but perhaps its true value was in all the minor new inventions that went into the final product. He broke new ground in multiple areas of engine design, precipitating many subsequent leaps in technology. Thanks to

Watt, engines could become smaller and more efficient at the same time. In 1804, just four years after Watt's patents died, Richard Trevithick designed the first steam locomotive. While these early models left much to be desired, it was only a matter of time before more great minds would join the endeavor and make railway transport a reality, changing the world forever. James Watt lived to see the blossoming of some of these new technologies before passing away at the age of 83 in 1819.

George Stephenson

For his outstanding feats in civil and mechanical engineering and his contributions to the development of railway infrastructure, George Stephenson is remembered as the Father of Railways. While James Watt perfected the engine, Stephenson ensured that Britain and humanity could use this technology for maximum benefit. The genius of George Stephenson was matched only by his unquenchable thirst for improvement, both in himself and in all things related to his work. Indeed, Stephenson was more than an inventor. He is also a reminder of the limitless potential that even a disadvantaged individual can unlock through sheer will and relentless self-improvement.

From Illiteracy to Science

Among the heroes of the Industrial Revolution, the story of how George Stephenson came up and made his name stands out as a particularly difficult journey. George was born on June 9, 1781, to illiterate, working-class parents in the English hamlet of Wylam. As can easily be imagined, life in the working class in those days must have been an eternal uphill battle by today's standards. George's father kept food on the table by working as a mechanic and operator of a Newcomen steam engine, pumping water out of a coal mine in Newcastle upon Tyne, some nine miles east of Wylam. Just like many other workers of the early industrial era, he earned a meager wage that was barely enough to sustain his family.

When George was born, the scenery of life in coal-mining villages was one of horses pulling wagons and carts loaded with coal since there were no locomotives in those days. This picture was one that the historic work done by the likes of James Watt and George Stephenson would eventually change. As a boy, however, George had virtually no prospects, but that was a circumstance he was committed to changing. George began working minor odd jobs when and where he could from the time he was a teenager. Witnessing the toils of his parents and foreseeing the same fate for himself in a cycle of poverty, George realized the value of education from the start. Unfortunately, his parents had no way of supporting an education.

For a time, George had to work in the mines as a laborer, but it wasn't long until he started moving up. Eventually, by the age of 19, he became a Newcomen operator like his father. He seemed to have a knack for repairing and maintaining engines and other mining equipment, which he did despite still being illiterate. While working, George attended a night school in order to learn basic mathematics and how to read and write, which unlocked new opportunities. On top of that, he picked up various trades, such as repairing shoes and clocks, to earn some additional income.

George Stephenson. [21]

George also got married around this time, which only further strengthened his resolve to spend every waking hour working hard and learning. After his wife died, George was left to care for his young son Robert on his own. He made sure that his boy attended school and would allocate time every day to help him with homework, with the hope that his son would never have to struggle as much as he did.

Father of the Railways

It all began in 1813 when George Stephenson was invited by John Blenkinsop to visit a nearby coal mine. Blenkinsop wanted George to take a look at his contraption, which he referred to as a steam boiler on wheels and used to carry coal from the mine. In principle, the idea was there, but this rudimentary improvisation was prone to breaking down. It featured a notched third wheel set on a cogged rail in the middle of the tracks. Blenkinsop made this addition to the system as a way of maximizing traction since he believed the regular wooden rails were too smooth for a machine of such weight.

Stephenson took a good look at this machine and, as was his nature, immediately asked himself how it might be improved. By that time, Stephenson had become the chief mechanic at the Killingworth coal mine, owned by Lord Ravensworth. Ravensworth had the means of supporting Stephenson's ideas and seeing them come to fruition. He was happy to do so, given George's reputation for being gifted in all things related to steam engines. The ensuing efforts resulted in Stephenson's construction of the Blucher, a locomotive capable of pulling eight full wagons at a speed of four miles per hour.

For Stephenson, this was but a prototype. He soon managed to increase the power of the engine by using a chimney as an exhaust, which increased the pull of air, with the subsequent draft essentially producing a blast. From then on, Stephenson continued building increasingly better and more practical engines, making him a minor legend in the coal mining industry.

He also came into the public eye after inventing his own safety lamp, which reduced the risk of explosions in the case of gas release within a mine. This invention stirred up controversy because Humphry Davy, a distinguished scientist, was working on the same problem. The two inventors presented their devices around the same time, and even though the designs were significantly different, Stephenson was accused of plagiarism, likely due to a lack of recognized scientific credentials to his name.

Stephenson's rise to fame as the Father of the Railways began in 1821 when he caught wind of a proposed railroad project connecting Stockton and Darlington. The project's idea was to use horses to transport coal along this railroad, which meant an enormous opportunity for Stephenson. He pitched his idea for a steam locomotive, impressing the project managers. Just four years later, 1825 marked the birth of a new mode of transport when Stephenson devised his Locomotion No. 1, initially called Active.

The implications of this groundbreaking, highly practical machine were incredible, making it clear that the train could do much more than haul coal. The line between Darlington and Stockton was soon opened for public transport, hosting the first passenger train in history. 450 people at once could now travel along the railway at an impressive 15 miles per hour. It wasn't long until George and his beloved son and partner Robert were commissioned for major railway projects, such as the 40-mile railroad between Liverpool and Manchester.

The father and son, since 1823, working as "Robert Stephenson and Company," were finalizing their work on the Liverpool-Manchester line in 1829. Before opening the line, they organized a locomotive competition to push the limits of speed. Unsurprisingly, George and Robert's new locomotive, the Rocket, blew everyone away at 36 miles per hour. The line was officially opened in September of 1830, and from that point on, railroad infrastructure would proliferate across the world at a breakneck speed. George Stephen continued building new machines and many other railways with his son whilst also working as a consultant on projects far and wide. He died on August 12, 1848, as an accomplished 67-year-old man who changed the world. George left behind a colossal legacy and a worthy successor in Robert, who would go on to be regarded by some as the greatest engineer of the 19th century.

Chapter 8: Charles Dickens and Florence Nightingale: Reform and Compassion

The long and eventful Victorian era was a defining period in modern British history. There are a few mainstream definitions of this period's time span, one of them being the long reign of Queen Victoria between 1837 and 1901. Due to this period's cultural, social, and political weight, there is also a wider definition, which places the Victorian era between 1820 and 1914. It was a period of growth for Britain in almost every way, especially in terms of politics and economy. Socioeconomic classes became more clearly defined, but the democratic process also developed, allowing voting rights for more people.

The Victorian Era was named after Queen Victoria. [22]

During the Victorian era, Britain became the global imperial superpower that is now widely remembered. All of this exponential growth, wealth, industrialization, and power facilitated further breakthroughs in culture, art, science, and much more. At the same time, the rapidly changing and industrialized Victorian society provided more room for people to devote their thoughts to matters of conscience and compassion. This was particularly evident in the emergence of modern nursing thanks to the efforts of Florence Nightingale and the widely popular novels and social critiques of Charles Dickens.

Charles Dickens

The name of Charles Dickens might not have the global reach of Shakespeare, but it's certainly close. However, in the Western world, especially the Anglosphere, Dickens enjoys a legendary status. Charles Dickens was also incredibly popular during his career, and he wisely used his fame and popularity to put forth insightful social critique through his work and various characters. He notably made clever use of plot devices like cliffhangers to entice readers and retain their interest in his serial writings. The works of Charles Dickens continue to be widely popular, read, and studied today. They provide valuable insight into the mentality and social dynamics of Victorian England while exploring themes that remain relevant in today's world.

The Early Years of the Greatest Victorian Novelist

The giant among humanity's novelists, famous for David Copperfield, Oliver Twist, A Tale of Two Cities, and many other masterpieces, was born on February 7, 1812, in the town of Portsmouth, located on Portsea Island. Charles' father, John Dickens, had a clerk's job with the Royal Navy, which would have afforded an Englishman a living wage in the Victorian era. However, John was notoriously irresponsible with his family's finances, which created many problems for his wife, Elizabeth, and their eight children.

The family would relocate a few times while Charles was very young, as his father's financial woes gradually devolved into an accumulation of debt. John was eventually incarcerated because of his indiscretions when Charles was only 12. Due to this difficult situation, Charles had to leave school and begin working before he even became a teenager. He took up a factory job at Warren's Blacking Warehouse, where he was tasked with sticking labels on packaged shoe polish, also called blacking.

Already a clever boy at age 12, Charles found his daily 10-hour shifts on this mind-numbing job positively excruciating, but he lasted around a year. He would remember this period as one of the worst times of his life. Things started looking up somewhat a couple of years later when his father was released from his term at the debtors' prison. His father's return alleviated some of the financial pressures, enabling Charles to partly continue attending school. This didn't last for long, though, and he resumed working when he was 15, this time employed on a menial job at an office.

Never content with menial work, Charles took what opportunities he could to work on himself and acquire new skills. While still a teenager, he learned to write in shorthand and would eventually qualify as a stenographer. This opened up new job opportunities, and Charles soon began working in the courts of London as a reporter. He did well as a reporter and subsequently managed to get hired by more than one newspaper in London in the early 1830s.

Writing as a newspaper reporter merely whetted Charles' appetite, however, and he soon found himself wanting to pursue his own path. His first independent steps as a writer were taken in the world of sketches, which he wrote and submitted to numerous magazines, newspapers, and other publications from 1883 onward. Dickens wrote and submitted his work under the nickname "Boz," which he used as a pseudonym. The sketches he wrote were short pieces revolving around the various shades of London life. As he recollected later, he was worried and afraid the first time he placed one of his manuscripts into a publication's letter box. He did so covertly and completely anonymously, dropping his submission and hoping for the best.

The first story he successfully published was A Dinner at Poplar Walk, accepted by The Monthly Magazine. Charles could hardly contain his excitement and described the feeling of seeing his work in a magazine as pure joy, as he knew that his life had turned a corner. Better yet, his little stories gradually amassed an audience of readers who developed a taste for his themes and style. After accumulating a number of successful submissions, Charles Dickens published his first collection in 1836, simply titled Sketches by "Boz." The illustrations in the collection were done by George Cruikshank, a rather accomplished illustrator and caricaturist at the time, as well as a friend of Dickens.

Success and Legacy

The personal experiences and hardships of his childhood and England's socioeconomic issues in the Victorian era permeate much of Charles Dickens' work. His difficult upbringing and early career didn't harden Charles' heart or provoke misanthropic tendencies. Quite to the contrary, Dickens infused a lot of his work with a notable degree of compassion for the working class, the poor, and the otherwise downtrodden.

The first collection of short works that Dickens published proved to be a considerable success, which opened up more publishing opportunities and allowed his career to start blooming. His further work with illustrations eventually evolved into The Pickwick Papers, which was Dickens' first published novel, published as a series between 1836 and 1837. Two years later, Oliver Twist came out.

Charles Dickens was a hard worker, and he made sure to build upon his successes at a rapid pace, publishing Nicholas Nickleby and The Old Curiosity Shop by 1841. Even though he had now established a steady career as a novelist, Dickens continued writing articles as a side venture. Dickens was more than popular, and it could be argued that his work caused a sensation. His ability to construct fascinating characters and weave a profoundly relative narrative of their lives resonated with the masses on a deeper level.

A lot of Dickens' work incorporated tragic aspects and just enough comic relief to keep people emotionally hooked and satisfied. His stories were

Charles Dickens. [23]

relatable because he had an insight into working-class life and possessed a keen ability to empathize with such people. The fates and difficult circumstances befalling his characters were something that many of his readers or someone they knew had experienced. Still, even those with no such background and no contact with that kind of life found Dickens' stories interesting because they offered a window into the world of a significant portion of the population in Victorian England.

Dickens' ability to create suspense through his serial work was also a huge help in keeping readers gripped by the stories. The publishers were happy to have a steady stream of highly popular material, and the audience was excited to see where the stories went. In a way, Dickens' works sometimes resemble the way television drama works in today's world. People engaged in speculation, discussed the latest developments with their friends and family, and eagerly waited for the next episode. Dickens' popularity soon reached beyond England, and he became internationally celebrated. In the early 1840s, Dickens took America by storm, solidifying him as an international star at the age of 30. When he visited America at that time, he received greetings and a warm welcome from fans far and wide.

In the 1840s, Dickens started getting socially involved as well, touring industrial areas, speaking before workers, and noting the socioeconomic inequalities of the time. The urge to address these issues spawned A Christmas Carol in late 1843, which would become one of his most beloved novels. He continued his travels and activism afterward, all while writing prolifically, publishing David Copperfield, Hard Times, Dombey and Son, and many more successful works. Through the 1850s, Dickens had amassed a considerable fortune and settled comfortably into his life as a public figure, often invited to do public readings.

Despite his success and riches, Dickens had problems in his personal life. He was embroiled in a scandal when he left his wife, with whom he had 10 children, and had an affair with Ellen Ternan, a young actress. Dickens' daughter Kate later said that her father and Ellen had a daughter who died as an infant. Apart from his broken home, some of his other personal relationships also suffered in the subsequent years, but Dickens did continue making a good living from his tours in the late stages of his life. Dickens died following a stroke in June of 1870 while working on The Mystery of Edwin Drood. Besides the fact that his work is widely enjoyed to this day, the true weight of its legacy is in the many adaptations and interpretations it has inspired in literature, theater, television, film, and many other art forms.

Florence Nightingale

Throughout most of the history of warfare, nurses have existed in one form or another to take care of the wounded, so it was certainly not a new concept in Victorian England. What was needed, however, was for someone to revolutionize it and turn nursing into a more organized, professional calling. Florence Nightingale became one of the greatest Victorian icons by doing precisely that. She was also an accomplished writer, gifted statistician, and social reformer who did much more than create the modern profession of nursing. She initially made her name during the Crimean War between 1853 and 1856 when she managed and trained nurses behind the front, but this was just the beginning of her many contributions that would produce tremendous positive effects on society as a whole.

The Awakening of the Lady with the Lamp

Florence Nightingale entered the world on May 12, 1820, born in her namesake city in Italy. She was born into a wealthy British family to William Edward and Frances Nightingale. The fact that she was born in Italy was somewhat accidental, as her parents were vacationing in Florence as part of their honeymoon. It was a prolonged honeymoon, and a few months would pass after Florence's birth until the Nightingales went back to England. Florence would spend most of her youthful years in two-family homes, including one in Derbyshire in central England and another in Embley, Hampshire.

As a young girl, Florence received an extensive education, particularly in languages, history, philosophy, and grammar. Contrary to gender conventions of the time and some minor resistance from her parents, Florence was also given tutorship in mathematics around the age of 20. She had a keen mind and a great thirst for intellectual pursuits. Instead of doing chores and receiving training in homemaking, Florence preferred to read philosophy and debate her father on politics and social issues. Apart from her education, Florence expressed an interest in humanitarian work and philanthropy when she was still a teenager. She often volunteered to help people who were sick, especially those who were poor.

As she later explained, February 7, 1837, was a decisive moment in her life because, on that day, she heard the voice of God. This was one of several such experiences, which she referred to as "calls from God." She explained that she had received a message urging her to devote her life to reducing the suffering of humanity. This mission was something that came naturally to Florence, and she soon realized that the best course would be to become a nurse. Despite her passion and her voluntary work before that point, Florence had difficulties in her attempts to enroll in a training program. This was primarily because her parents didn't want her to pursue a nurse's calling, which was a path they saw as too low for their daughter and her social class.

Florence also expressed no interest in marriage, rejecting a proposal by Richard Monckton Milnes, whom she actually liked. Even though she considered him suitable, Florence told him that her calling was to pursue a mission that lay beyond traditional life at home. Her family's objections ultimately proved futile, and Florence was able to enroll at the Institution of Protestant Deaconesses in Germany in the early 1850s.

A Legacy of Care

After a short while working close to Paris, she returned to England in 1853 and began working as a nurse at the Institution for the Care of Sick Gentlewomen in London. Her education and the burning passion she had for the job quickly made Florence stand out, soon earning her the position of superintendent at the institution. Despite having her hands full, she also volunteered elsewhere, notably at a hospital in Middlesex. This was where she first tackled the problem of terrible hygienic standards. She fought tooth and nail to introduce reforms to change the unsanitary conditions contributing to the hospital's cholera outbreak. By introducing new practices and elevating hygiene, Florence considerably reduced the outbreak's death rate.

Florence Nightingale. [24]

Florence made a big name for herself through her service in the Crimean War, which started in October of 1853. This war on the Black Sea pitted the British Empire and its allies against Russia. Apart from this war, the Victorian era was largely peaceful for Britain, at least in great power politics. As such, the public watched the news from the front with close interest, and attention was soon brought to the lack of standards in medical care for the wounded and sick. Hearing the stories of wounded British fighters being kept in horrifyingly unsanitary hospitals enraged the public. Florence knew that something must be done, setting out for the Ottoman Empire in 1854 with 38 other nurses in her charge.

When the nurses reached the war zone, they quickly realized that Russian bullets and shells were the least of the problems facing wounded British troops. The hospital Florence was assigned to was horrific, with contamination from a nearby cesspool polluting the water supply, feces-smeared hospital beds, a scarcity of bandages and soap, and rampant disease outbreaks. Soldiers were dying left and right from preventable causes simply due to horrendous hospital standards.

The work to be done was tremendous, but Florence would not let up until the hospital was thoroughly reformed. It wasn't long until she became an administrator rather than just a nurse. She coordinated, raised funds, organized the staff, and still kept helping the soldiers on an individual level. The time she spent around the hospital in the night earned her the famous "Lady with the Lamp" moniker. According to some estimates, in the first six months since her arrival, Florence was able to get the hospital's mortality rate from 60% down to 2%.

Florence used her skills as a statistician to keep track of her success, and some of her work affected the later methods of data visualization, such as the widely-used pie chart. During her time at the front, Florence was unaware of the reputation she had attained back home. When she returned after the war in the summer of 1856, she was a heroine. More important than public adoration was the institutional recognition and backing she could now get for future projects. Grants started coming in, and Florence got busy writing important papers, establishing hospitals, and running training programs for nurses.

Her writings and reforms changed the profession forever and led to widespread reforms in public and military healthcare institutions. Unfortunately, Florence fell ill with brucellosis during her time in Turkey. Around the age of 38, her health began to deteriorate and would be a problem for the rest of her life. Even though she often couldn't leave her home, Florence continued her hard work, making many other revolutionary contributions to medicine by the time she died on August 13, 1910.

Chapter 9: Leadership Through the Lens of World War II

When it comes to the more recent history of England and the United Kingdom, there are few names that ring out as loudly as that of Winston Churchill. It would hardly be an exaggeration to say that he is among the most famous British people to have ever lived. Churchill's political career spanned at least half a century, but he was politically involved and active much longer than that without always holding a political office.

The career of Winston Churchill is a historical era of its own, covering some of the most monumental shifts in British and

Winston Churchill.[25]

world history. From the heyday of British imperial power and colonial dominion over both world wars to the height of the Cold War when Britain declined as a key global player, Churchill saw it all. Many other people witnessed the same things, but Churchill was one of the very few who often played a key role and steered the destiny of not just the UK but the entire world. Such a long and eventful career in politics could not go by without its controversies, though, and Churchill certainly stirred up his fair share. In fact, he does so to this day, decades after his departure.

A Soldier and Politician of the Empire

Winston Churchill rose to prominence in an era when Britain had long settled into its parliamentary system. In previous centuries, true power usually rested with the monarch and his nobles, but in Churchill's time, many other powerful political offices had long been established. The power that Churchill would wield through some of these offices, particularly as prime minister, was highly indicative of how much the monarchy had changed and evolved since the old days in medieval Europe.

Early Life and Career

It is fair to assess that Winston Churchill was set up for success and expected to do great things right from the start, although he would eventually take a path that deviated from what was expected of him. He was born Winston Leonard Spencer Churchill on November 30, 1874, at his family's estate in Blenheim, not far from Oxfordshire. His father, Lord Randolph Churchill, descended from an extensive line of aristocracy and politics. Lord Randolph was a politician, too, making a considerable name for himself as a member of the Conservative Party (Tories) during the 1870s and 1880s.

Winston was partly of American descent through his mother, Jennie Jerome. She also came from America's closest equivalent of aristocracy, as her father was a wealthy businessman and investor. Churchill attended a prep school called Harrow, but even in his early school years, it was apparent that studies weren't his strong suit. Apart from poor grades, young Churchill's behavior was also less than ideal. Having very slim prospects of attending prestigious universities like Oxford or Cambridge, Churchill was steered by his father toward a military career. It took three attempts for him to be accepted into the Royal Military College, Sandhurst, and his career in the armed forces finally began in 1893.

Despite his difficulties in getting admitted to military school, Churchill performed surprisingly well for a youth with a known streak of rebelliousness and misbehavior. Impressively enough, he was eventually 20th in a class of 130 when he graduated. When Churchill entered active service as a young soldier, the United Kingdom of Great Britain and Ireland, as it was known in the 19th century, was at the height of imperial power. Even though Britain was largely at peace with other great powers after the Napoleonic Wars, there was never any shortage of skirmishes and limited local warfare aimed at colonial expansion. A young serviceman at that time could have the opportunity to travel the whole world and was very likely to experience at least limited combat somewhere in the vast British Empire.

Starting in 1895, Churchill's brief period of service in the Fourth Queen's Own Hussars saw him deployed at the frontier in India and Sudan. Churchill participated in the Battle of Omdurman in 1898, which gave him valuable combat experience. Churchill also worked as a journalist throughout his military career, publishing war reports for the Daily Telegraph and Pioneer Mail. He left active service in 1899, having already gone to war and written two books.

His departure from the army was in great part motivated by a strong desire to get involved in politics, but on the whole, Churchill continued working as a war correspondent, mostly writing for the Morning Post. This job saw him spending time in South Africa during the Second Boer War. It was during this assignment that Churchill had his first run-in with fame and glory after he was captured by the Boers and managed to escape, crossing some 300 miles in the process. This event attracted a lot of attention and made headlines across British publications. London to Ladysmith via Pretoria, a book he published in 1900, details these experiences.

Politics and World War I

Churchill was still a Tory when he entered the British parliament in 1900. Perhaps unexpectedly for some, Churchill devoted much of his early career to social reforms, especially regarding economics. His commitment to social justice saw him part ways with the Tories in 1904 since he felt that they weren't devoted to such ideas. After moving to the Liberal Party in 1904, it took another four years for Churchill to get a seat in the parliament with his new party. Shortly thereafter, he managed to get an appointment in the prime minister's cabinet, serving as the president of the Board of Trade.

Quite unbecoming of his militaristic and wartime legacies, Churchill used his new office to oppose larger investments in the Royal Navy. Instead, he focused on reforming the prison system and was instrumental in establishing a minimum wage in Britain. His other pursuits included unemployment insurance and increased taxes on the rich. Unfortunately, although it had previously been passed by the House of Commons, the tax increase, submitted to the parliament as the People's Budget, didn't make it past the House of Lords.

As a politician, Winston Churchill didn't shy away from spectacle. In a particularly noteworthy episode in early 1911, he intervened in a standoff between the police and two armed robbers who were under siege by law enforcement. According to some accounts, Churchill assisted in the decision-making during the siege and allegedly encouraged the firefighters not to intervene after the building was engulfed in flames. The suspects were later found to have been incinerated, but it's unclear to what extent Churchill's guidance influenced the fire brigade's decision to let the building burn down.

Churchill also got married to Clementine Ogilvy Hozier in 1908, finding in her a lifelong partner and a marriage that lasted 56 years. The couple would have five children over the years, losing one of them to illness at a very young age. The next important post that Churchill held was as First Lord of the Admiralty, to which he was appointed in October 1911. In this position, Churchill began to advocate new investments in the Royal Navy, particularly its modernization programs. As World War I neared, numerous countries started to experiment with combat aircraft and gradually formed their air forces. Churchill spearheaded such initiatives in the UK, contributing to the establishment of the Royal Navy

Clementine Hozier.[26]

Air Service and also taking a pilot's course while at it.

As Europe plunged into the Great War, Churchill was still in his Admiralty post, where he would experience the first major setback of his career. After the disastrous defeat of the UK and its allies in the Gallipoli campaign against the Ottoman Empire, Churchill was forced to resign in late 1915 for his part of the blame. This wouldn't be the end of his contribution to the war effort, though, as he soon joined the army and was deployed to the Western Front. He was then reassigned and became Minister of Munitions, where he would serve between 1917 and 1919, in charge of British military production.

The interwar period was one of the more controversial periods of Churchill's career regarding his legacy, particularly during his time as the Secretary of State for the Colonies in 1921 and 1922. This was a time when his adherence to imperialism came to the forefront and would remain a feature of his politics for quite a while to come. During the British suppression of a Kurdish revolt in Iraq, which had fallen under British control following the defeat of the Ottomans in World War I, Churchill was in favor of drastic solutions. He argued that chemical weapons should be used to quell the revolt, but these ideas didn't come to fruition. Churchill was also a supporter of Zionism early on, allowing Jewish immigration into British-controlled Mandatory Palestine before restricting the flow of migrants when ethno-religious tensions in Palestine began intensifying.

In 1922, Churchill left the Liberal Party and returned to the Conservatives, serving in their government for the next few years. His political career would hit a low point when the Tories lost their majority in 1929, which meant that Churchill also lost his seat. He described the 1920s as his most trying time, during which he would occupy his mind with painting, producing hundreds of pieces in the process. Churchill spent much of the 1930s mostly outside of politics, focusing on personal pursuits like writing.

The growing Indian independence movement rallied around Mahatma Gandhi, reinvigorating Churchill's interest in politics. His disdain for Gandhi and disparaging remarks toward Indians in general are well-known, and Churchill was one of the staunchest opponents of India's independence. As Hitler's Germany geared up for war and began absorbing its neighbors in the late 1930s, it became increasingly clear that fate wanted Winston Churchill to become active in politics again.

World War II and Beyond

Churchill led the United Kingdom through all the historic moments of World War II, from the important victory in the Battle of Britain to Operation Overlord and the decisive conferences of the Allies in Tehran and Yalta. For his relentless commitment to victory, aggressive demeanor, and ability to fire up the people, he earned the moniker of "British Bulldog," although his appearance certainly contributed to the nickname.

World War II was a time of unspeakable trials and tribulations for the entire world, so Churchill wasn't the only historical figure whose myth and legend were made in that war. Tough times have a way of filtering out the indecisive and the ill-prepared, though, and Churchill would prove his ability to stand the tests of those hard years of war, making his World War II legacy undoubtedly well-earned.

The British Bulldog

Strategic planning and decision-making aside, Churchill's biggest accomplishment was his ability to rally the people and inspire his nation to stand up to a very powerful enemy. Things looked grim in the opening stages of the Battle of Britain, but Churchill's indomitable spirit and his unshakable belief in victory were infectious.

During the first few years after the Nazis took over Germany, like many of his contemporaries, Churchill was somewhat complacent and ambivalent towards Hitler. However, once Germany's massive rearmament and growing militarism could no longer be ignored, Churchill realized that Britain should prepare. Seeing as he had no power at that time, Churchill could only criticize those in charge, most notably Prime Minister Neville Chamberlain.

Referred to in historiography as the policy of appeasement, Chamberlain's strategy was to avoid war at all costs, hoping that Germany would de-escalate its expansionism if given enough concessions at the expense of its weaker neighbors. Churchill and a growing number of other critics felt that this approach was a terrible mistake. When Britain declared war on Germany in the wake of its invasion of Poland in early September of 1939, the time came once again for Churchill to make his mark. He initially resumed his post as First Lord of the Admiralty, and in April of 1940, he chaired the Military Coordinating Committee.

At this point, the conflict between Churchill and Chamberlain escalated, centered on the prime minister's refusal to follow Churchill's advice and preemptively invade Norway ahead of the German northward push. Whether or not this was sound advice is a matter of debate, but Chamberlain continued resisting the idea. Sure enough, the Germans swept across Norway in April. Chamberlain resigned in May, at which point George VI of England put Churchill in his place and also made him Minister of Defense.

Churchill settled into his role as the leader of the war effort decisively and quickly. His assertive nature and a natural knack for leadership were fortunate for Britain because it was mere hours after his appointment that Hitler began moving his armies into the Low Countries, inching ever closer to the English Channel. France was invaded in short order as well, leading to a catastrophic initial defeat for the Western Allies and the famous evacuation from Dunkirk. Churchill proved to be a strong manager, bringing together leaders of all the major parties and seemingly always choosing the right man for the job in his appointments.

As he galvanized the entire nation to face an imminent threat, Churchill made history with his dramatic speeches to the parliament throughout the lead-up to the Battle of Britain. A historic moment was the speech he gave to the House of Commons on May 13, 1940, in which Churchill humbly professed that all he could offer were "blood, toil, tears, and sweat," warning of an imminent, hard battle while also stressing the existential necessity of victory. This address struck a perfect balance between foreboding and hopeful while also reminding that the United Kingdom and the world were faced with "a monstrous tyranny," whose evil he described as unprecedented in the history of mankind's crimes. This attitude fostered a readiness for hardship, a focus on victory, and contempt for a terrible enemy, all of which were essential ingredients to mobilize.

Following the successful evacuation of British and Allied troops from Dunkirk on June 4, Churchill gave another iconic performance before the House of Commons, the unforgettable "We shall fight on the beaches" address. This speech also served to additionally encourage the fighting spirit of the people in the face of a massive military setback that happened in France, but Churchill also took the opportunity to encourage the United States to lend its strength to the Allied cause.

The Battle of Britain monument. [37]

The Battle of Britain, which lasted between July 10 and October 31, 1940, was a turning point for the British war effort and quite possibly the entire world. It was merely an air and naval engagement above and around Britain, but it meant much more in the grand scheme of things. Had Hitler managed to subdue or completely knock Britain out, he would have secured the entire Western Front, allowing Germany to allocate most of its resources to the horrendous war in the East, which was yet to begin at that time.

The British ultimately prevailed, and the home islands were largely secured from that point on, although Germany continued a campaign of terror bombing for quite some time. American aid started to pour in from 1941 onward, and Washington entered the war later that year. The USSR also managed to survive the German onslaught and stabilized the front just short of complete disaster, owed in large part to heroic resistance but also assisted with massive shipments of weapons and equipment from the Western Allies. Thus, the tripartite core of the Allied war effort was consolidated and poised to take the fight to the enemy. Following the German defeats at Stalingrad and Kursk, the writing was on the wall for Hitler, but it was the massive Allied invasion of Normandy on June 6, 1944, that sealed the Third Reich's fate. Unfortunately, a lot more souls had to perish before the final surrender in May of 1945.

Later Years and Legacy

Churchill continued to prove his fine coordination skills on the international stage as well, being able to see eye-to-eye and make strategic plans with both Roosevelt and Stalin. Through the battles waged and the conferences held, Churchill was one of the three key players in shaping the Allied war effort – but also the *post-war world order*. As World War II entered its conclusion, things quickly fell apart between the Western block and the Soviets, and the rest is very recent history.

In the aftermath, it seemed almost as if Britain had no use for its legendary war leader after peace returned to Europe, and Churchill promptly lost the election in July of 1945. He was also one of the first Western politicians to officially announce the beginning of the Cold War when he gave the iconic speech about the Iron Curtain descending over Europe in 1946. He also advocated what some call British Atlanticism, a loosely defined political philosophy that promoted Britain's independence from pan-European political projects and a close relationship with Washington. It could be argued that this attitude made a bombastic return in 2016 with Britain's departure from the EU.

Churchill made a short return to government as prime minister and minister of defense in the early 1950s, during which time he focused again on social reforms whilst also having to contend with Britain's unquestionable decline as an imperial power. 1953 brought him knighthood at the Sword of Elizabeth II and a Nobel Prize for Literature. Winston Churchill concluded his incredibly eventful life on January 24, 1965, at 90 years of age. Accomplished in virtually all fields he would enter, he left behind a legacy for the ages. While that legacy is weighed down somewhat by his relentless commitment to old imperialism, he is primarily remembered as one of the people who defeated Nazism.

Chapter 10: Queen Elizabeth II and the Beatles

On the surface, Queen Elizabeth II and the Beatles don't seem to have much in common. The former was and still is a world-famous representative of England's long regal traditions and a window into a millennium of history. The Beatles, on the other hand, were renowned artists and, in many ways, the embodiment of counterculture in the intense '60s.

However, the queen and Britain's most illustrious musical group each played crucial roles in helping England find its place in a rapidly changing world and shaping the nation's global image. They also

Queen Elizabeth II. [28]

allowed England to cross the bridge between the past and present and position itself as an important human center well into the post-imperial era.

The Longest-Reigning British Monarch

Over the centuries, the function and role of the English and, subsequently, British monarchs have evolved a great deal. As Britain delved further into a system of parliamentary monarchy and democracy, many of the old powers of the monarch would be curtailed, turning it into a largely ceremonial role. The long reign of Elizabeth II, which lasted from 1952 to 2022, illustrated that the lack of raw executive powers once possessed by the monarchy didn't necessarily mean less influence.

In today's post-colonial world, soft power has proven to be an essential feature of worldly influence, and Elizabeth II was the embodiment of this principle. She also demonstrated that Britain had entered a new era with a firm understanding of this philosophy, proving itself as one of the most adaptable and resilient monarchies in human history. As British hard power waned in the era of decolonization and the Cold War between two new superpowers, the omnipresence of Elizabeth II in the world helped Britain retain its position as one of the key centers of influence.

Early Life, Family, and Marriage

While Elizabeth II's time on the throne spanned the majority of the Cold War and decades in the post-Cold War world, her life also saw much of the previous era. The longevity of her reign is surpassed only by her long and eventful lifetime, which spanned four quite distinct epochs of recent world history. Born in 1926 in Mayfair, London, Elizabeth was raised during the interwar period in a world that was vastly different than the world of today. In her youth, she witnessed the monumental events of World War II and the years in its aftermath, all before becoming queen.

The queen was born Elizabeth Alexandra Mary of House Windsor on April 21, to George VI of England and Elizabeth Bowes-Lyon. The title she was born into was Princess of York, and there wasn't much likelihood of her becoming queen later in life. Her only sibling was her younger sister, Princess Margaret, but her father was George V's younger son. Edward VIII, Elizabeth's uncle, inherited George V's throne in 1936 and was set to establish a line of succession, but he abdicated only 326 days into his reign, having produced no heirs by that point. Thus, Elizabeth's father assumed the throne, so fate opened a door for the eldest of his two daughters. George VI ruled until his death on February 6, 1952, and Elizabeth II of England soon became the new monarch.

As was customary for most young royals, Elizabeth's childhood was filled with nannies, tutors, and various instructors, who spent more time with her than her parents. However, this didn't prevent her from having a solid relationship with them, especially her mother. Elizabeth Bowes-Lyon was a pious Christian woman who ensured that her daughter inherited the same values. Apart from faith, young Elizabeth's mother also exalted the virtues of responsibility and duty, teaching her everything she needed to know about being part of the royal family. Elizabeth and her sister also learned a lot from their grandmother, queen, and consort, Mary.

As a young princess, Elizabeth was instructed on a number of subjects that royalty should master, including history, law, arts, horse riding, and French as a second language. It was during this time that Elizabeth became an avid horse enthusiast, which was one of her more famous traits during her time as queen. Breeding and keeping pristine racehorses became a hobby of hers, but she was also a dog lover and owner with a particular penchant for corgis.

World War II was another period of intense learning for Elizabeth, just as it was for everyone else. It was also a time when she began to acquire more experience with her duties as a member of royalty. For most of World War II, especially during the Battle of Britain, Elizabeth and her sister were relocated to Windsor Castle, an almost millennium-old fortress not far from London. During this time, the princess was acquainted with the military and its functions, being given an honorary colonel rank in the Royal Army by her father. In the late stages of the war, she also held a seat on the Privy Council and the Council of State, which were significant responsibilities, leaving her in charge of certain functions at times when the king was preoccupied with other matters.

Elizabeth's 1947 engagement to Prince Philip of Greece, Duke of Edinburgh, was another important milestone in her life. Some in the royal family were less than impressed with the prince's pedigree, which indicates that this was a marriage of love. The royal wedding was held on November 20 at Westminster Abbey, and it wasn't long until Elizabeth's first son and heir, Charles, was born. The couple would have three more children by 1964, including Princess Anne, Prince Andrew, and Prince Edward, all of whom are well-known members of the royal family nowadays. Thanks to the longevity of both Elizabeth and Philip, their marriage lasted for an impressive 73 years. Philip was 99 when he died in 2021.

The British Crown in a New Era

The time for Elizabeth to assume the throne came in 1952 when her father died prematurely at 56 due to lung cancer. His health had already been on a decline before that point, so Elizabeth had begun taking on a growing number of responsibilities in 1951. Elizabeth II was formally crowned at Westminster Abbey on June 2, 1953. At that time, Winston Churchill was fulfilling his second tenure as prime minister. It wasn't long until the young queen would face her first major challenges, starting with the Suez Crisis of 1956.

The Suez Crisis was a major turning point not just for Elizabeth II but for the United Kingdom as a global power. It marked the unquestionable decline of Britain as a major global superpower, as it became evident that the Cold War order would be dominated by Washington and Moscow. The crisis was a major foreign policy blow for London, and the queen wasn't exempt from criticism in the immediate aftermath. This was when Elizabeth changed her focus and began working to adapt the image of Britain and the crown to a changing world.

Elizabeth would eventually become something of a people's queen, focusing intently on her image and making sure she was present in public life beyond politics. For instance, she was an early adopter of televised addresses, starting with a Christmas broadcast in 1957. Two decades later, Elizabeth marked her Silver Jubilee, or 25 years of rule, with an extensive tour around the Commonwealth.

Prince Charles and Princess Diana. [29]

Unfortunately for the queen, her image and that of the royal family wasn't always in her hands alone. The controversially dysfunctional marriage between her son Charles and Lady Diana Spencer was a source of discomfort for the whole family throughout the '80s and '90s. Even though the marriage fell apart, it birthed William and Harry, who are some of the most famous young British royals today. Also, in the '90s, the royal family was under intense public scrutiny over spending. Elizabeth wisely addressed the controversy by voluntarily paying taxes that she didn't have to by law. While this was a small dent in her vast royal estate, the decision resonated with the public. Another strategy to bring the royal family closer to the people was to allow public access to Buckingham Palace.

One of the most controversial episodes of Elizabeth II's reign was the 1997 death of Princess Diana. Lady Diana was widely beloved among the people of Britain and beyond, which is what made the divorce from Charles particularly tricky for the royal family. Her death sparked a firestorm of grief and outrage on a large scale. Many of Diana's fans already felt that the royal family had mistreated the princess, so Elizabeth had to tread carefully after Diana's death in Paris. A televised address to the nation was arranged, and the queen had a number of personal meetings regarding Diana. Flags on the Buckingham Palace were lowered to half-mast in mourning. 2.5 billion people watched the televised funeral, and although Diana's death sparked endless debates and theories, the grief was eventually overcome.

At 70 years, Elizabeth II's reign was the longest by a considerable margin, followed by the rule of Victoria, which lasted over 63 years. Elizabeth II also lived the longest, passing away at the ripe old age of 96. To say that she lived an impressive, eventful life is a severe understatement, and her life has been very well documented. Apart from ruling the United Kingdom, Elizabeth II was also the reigning monarch of the Commonwealth, which included 53 nations at its height, mostly comprised of territories once belonging to the vast British colonial empire.

Elizabeth II's time on the throne was marked by consistently high popularity among the people despite a number of scandals, which is more than can be said for some of the other members of the royal family. Even when other royals were involved in scandals that slashed their ratings with the public, this did little to harm the reputation of the queen. She was also a highly proactive monarch, content to fulfill her ceremonial role but never failing to make the most of it. Indeed, Elizabeth II's relatively limited powers were hardly an obstacle preventing her from taking on an active role in politics both at home and abroad.

Queen Elizabeth II died on September 8, 2022. She continued carrying out many of her duties right until the very end and remained highly active in both work and leisure. The royal family's reputational setbacks of the 1990s seemed like a distant memory by that point, as they had enjoyed a considerable increase in popularity throughout the 21st century. Elizabeth II passed away as a popular, accomplished monarch, finally succeeded by her son Charles III, crowned on May 6, 2023.

The Cultural Phenomenon of the Beatles

The Beatles need no introduction, but their history and unprecedented influence very much warrant deeper exploration. It was already clear during their heyday that the Beatles were something special, but the historical perspective of today shines an even brighter light on just how big of a phenomenon this band was. The significance of the Beatles is about much more than the fame they attained and the effect that they had on their generation of music. Their legacy is a symbol of English cultural influence in the world at a time when Britain's political power seemed to be waning.

If Queen Elizabeth II demonstrated England's ability to preserve its traditions and adapt them to survive in a rapidly changing world, then the Beatles showed that England could also continue to influence the world in a profound way. The Beatles also represented a much wider human current and encapsulated an entire cultural zeitgeist during the height of the Cold War, attaining a level of relevance and admiration that was much bigger than any one country or nation.

A Brief History and an Endless Legacy

If a chronicle of the history and life of the Beatles were to start at the very beginning, it would have to begin during the Blitz. Only about a month after German bombs began raining down on Britain, John Winston Lennon was born on October 9, 1940, in Liverpool. There is certainly a degree of poetry in the fact that one of the people who would redefine British culture and mark an entire era was born during a period that also left an enormous imprint on modern English history.

John Lennon showed a deep interest in music from a young age, especially American rock and roll, which was taking the world by storm in the 1950s. Already in 1956, when Lennon was just a teenager, he was looking to form a band with like-minded aspiring musicians in Liverpool.

He took his first steps by forming the Blackjacks in 1956, around a year before meeting Paul McCartney, a fellow rock and roll enthusiast. It wasn't long after meeting that they started playing together, and in 1957, McCartney joined Lennon's skiffle group as a rhythm guitarist. By that time, the band was known as the Quarrymen.

George Harrison joined the following year, recommended and invited by McCartney. Thus, the nucleus of what would become the Beatles was consolidated in the ensuing months as it essentially went through a spontaneous filtering process. Most of Lennon's friends from school who had been playing with the Quarrymen since the beginning gradually left, but Lennon, McCartney, and Harrison decided to stick together and maintain the chemistry.

The band then went through various changes, using a few different names, such as the Silver Beetles and Silver Beatles, until settling for just The Beatles in the summer of 1960. This simplified, clever name was the idea of the band's first bass guitarist, Stuart Sutcliffe, who passed away in 1962 when he was just 21. The fourth core member of the famous lineup, Ringo Starr, joined the band shortly after.

Even though they were still a small band mostly known locally in Liverpool, the Beatles got a significant boost in August of 1960 when Allan Williams helped them perform in Germany. Their stay ended up much longer than initially intended and would set the stage for their international acclaim. Another key player in setting the band up for success and shaping their image was Brian Epstein. 1962 was also the first time the Beatles performed live on television.

The Beatles. [80]

Things really took off in 1963 when the Beatles released Please Please Me, their debut LP, an album that Lennon was personally unhappy with, lambasting the concept and the lyrics. However, the public paid no attention to Lennon's self-critique, as the "Please Please Me" single topped the UK charts. The band's rise to prominence was staggering and swift. They blitzed through the press and the public, quickly becoming a phenomenon, with journalists throwing around new terms such as "Beatlemania." This was just the beginning, though, as the blazing boy band would consecutively have ten more number-one UK albums. When the Beatles' influence expanded into the massive US market that year, there was truly no stopping the train.

The band touched down in New York in February of 1964, mobbed by thousands of fans and the press. An example of just how popular they had become in the US was their televised American debut on The Ed Sullivan Show, which drew in around 34% of the American population. Almost overnight, the youth of America and beyond wanted to talk, look, and act like the Beatles. Not content to just settle into their boy band role and lazily reap the rewards, the Beatles would continue to forge ahead with their art well after blowing up. The lasting legacy of their experimental Sgt. Pepper's Lonely Hearts Club Band album perfectly exemplifies the band's desire to not just make music but also shape it.

The music was just one part of the story, as the band, particularly John Lennon, wanted to affect the world in other ways. The band is associated with so many timeless '60s moments that it would be exceedingly difficult to list them all. Lennon never shied away from speaking his mind and championing a cause when he felt he had to do the right thing.

The Beatles had some well-known run-ins with racial segregation during their touring across the US, which Lennon found particularly jarring. On September 11, 1964, the Beatles threatened to cancel a performance in Jacksonville, Florida, when they heard the audience would be racially segregated. The demand for the Beatles was so frenzied that the city backed down and heeded the band's demand to integrate the audience.

The rest is history, as the public presence and influence of the Beatles in the second half of the 1960s is a renowned historical epoch that is still very fresh in memory. The Beatles were adored, controversial, outrageous, and almost deified. Their music and public escapades changed the cultural landscape of the UK, the US, and much of the world forever. Lennon was particularly consequential in the anti-war movement during the Vietnam era, and his contribution to the rise of hippie culture was immense. To this day, similar movements and trends rarely emerge without referencing John Lennon as an inspiration to some extent.

There was hardly a social convention or institution that Lennon wouldn't question or irritate at some point, once infamously remarking that the Beatles were more popular than Christ. However, the Beatles were only human in the end, and the band broke up in 1970 after a period of personal friction and disagreements, particularly between Lennon and McCartney. The core band members would continue their music careers well after the dissolution of the Beatles, with McCartney and Ringo remaining active to this day. Lennon met a tragic end on December 8, 1980, at the hands of a disgruntled fan by the name of Mark David Chapman. Death only cemented the immortality of Lennon's work, leaving behind a legacy that will outlive the centuries.

Conclusion

The historical figures summarized in this book are only a fraction of all the essential people who have written the pages of English and British history, but they do have a somewhat distinct narrative role. Namely, they personify all those crucial steps and milestones that a nation must go through on its path of consolidation and development. As different as they and their roles were, and despite the fact that their lives spanned almost a thousand years, they are all connected on a fundamental level.

Medieval monarchs laid the foundations of the English state. Religious leaders shaped the monarchy's spiritual direction and ways of worship. Artists defined their culture and creativity. Scientists and inventors introduced technology and transformed the economy. Philosophers guided further moral development and political schools of thought. All of these people and their pursuits are the essential parts of one big whole, defining English identity and making it what it is today.

If only one of the epoch-defining characters discussed in this book were to be somehow erased from history, England would be a much different nation. As such, England itself is the collective legacy of all the great icons that make up its history. That is why these great minds, leaders, and pioneers are all intimately connected to contemporary England with an unbreakable thread of continuity.

That same thread will continue weaving its way into the future for centuries to come, which is why it's essential to be mindful of history. Only by learning from the triumphs and failures of history can the current generation fulfill its purpose as a bridge between past generations and those that will come in the future. The inheritance of experience and knowledge across generations is the quintessential human trait that makes civilizational advances possible. England and the rest of the world will continue to develop and change over time for as long as history progresses. Keeping the thread of history unbroken will ensure that this evolution chugs along as smoothly as possible, informed by both the lessons and mistakes of the past.

Check out another book in the series

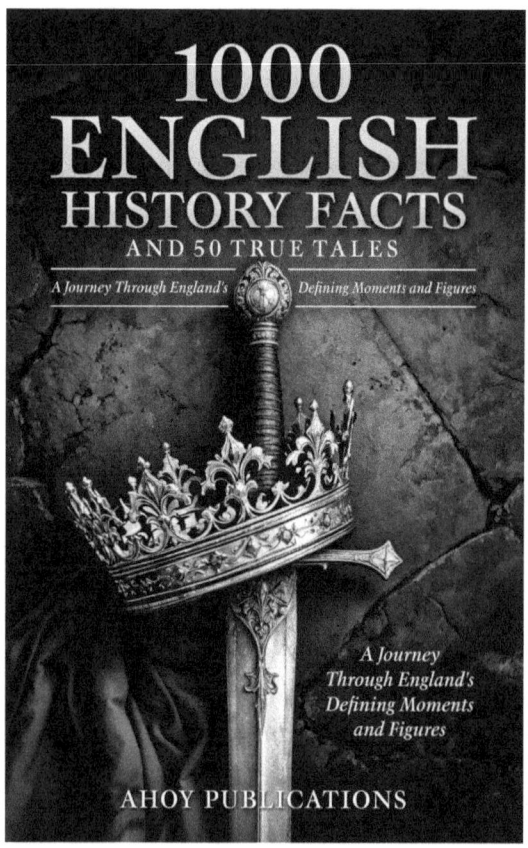

Welcome Aboard, Check Out This Limited-Time Free Bonus!

Ahoy, reader! Welcome to the Ahoy Publications family, and thanks for snagging a copy of this book! Since you've chosen to join us on this journey, we'd like to offer you something special.

Check out the link below for a FREE e-book filled with delightful facts about American History.

But that's not all - you'll also have access to our exclusive email list with even more free e-books and insider knowledge. Well, what are ye waiting for? Click the link below to join and set sail toward exciting adventures in American History.

Access your bonus here
https://ahoypublications.com/
Or, Scan the QR code!

Sources and Additional References

Part 1: English History Trivia

Schama, Simon. *A History of Britain: At the Edge of the World? 3000 BC–AD 1603*. New York: Hyperion, 2000.

Ackroyd, Peter. *Foundation: The History of England from Its Earliest Beginnings to the Tudors*. New York: Thomas Dunne Books, 2011.

Douglas, David C., and George W. Greenaway, eds. *English Historical Documents*. London: Eyre & Spottiswoode, various volumes and years.

Elton, G. R. *England Under the Tudors*. London: Methuen, 1955.

Fraser, Antonia. *The Lives of the Kings and Queens of England*. Berkeley: University of California Press, 1975.

Part 2: Notable Figures in English History

Bellis, M. (2017, March 6). What Do You Know about the Guy Who Invented the Steam Locomotive Engine? ThoughtCo. https://www.thoughtco.com/history-of-the-railroad-1992457

Bellis, M. (2020, April 27). Biography of James Watt, Inventor of the Modern Steam Engine. ThoughtCo. https://www.thoughtco.com/james-watt-inventor-of-the-modern-steam-engine-1992685

Biography.com Editors. (2021, January 22). Winston Churchill – Quotes, Paintings & Death. Biography. https://www.biography.com/political-figures/winston-churchill

Cartwright, M. (2019a, January 30). William the Conqueror. World History Encyclopedia. https://www.worldhistory.org/William_the_Conqueror/

Cartwright, M. (2019b, December 10). Henry II of England. World History Encyclopedia. https://www.worldhistory.org/Henry_II_of_England/

Cartwright, M. (2020, May 26). Elizabeth I of England. World History Encyclopedia. https://www.worldhistory.org/Elizabeth_I_of_England/

Cartwright, M. (2020a, March 10). Thomas Becket. World History Encyclopedia. https://www.worldhistory.org/Thomas_Becket/

Cartwright, M. (2020b, April 9). Henry VIII of England. World History Encyclopedia. https://www.worldhistory.org/Henry_VIII_of_England/

Cartwright, M. (2023, November 21). John Locke. World History Encyclopedia. https://www.worldhistory.org/John_Locke/

Cartwright, M. (2023a, September 19). Isaac Newton. World History Encyclopedia. https://www.worldhistory.org/Isaac_Newton/

Cartwright, M. (2023b, September 21). Robert Hooke. World History Encyclopedia. https://www.worldhistory.org/Robert_Hooke/

Cartwright, M. (2023c, November 8). Scientific Revolution. World History Encyclopedia. https://www.worldhistory.org/Scientific_Revolution/

Christopher Marlowe – Plays, Works & Doctor Faustus. (2020, July 28). Biography. https://www.biography.com/authors-writers/christopher-marlowe

Editors. (2016, July 8). Elizabeth I and the Build-up to the Spanish Armada 1588 | Royal Museums Greenwich. Www.rmg.co.uk. https://www.rmg.co.uk/stories/blog/curatorial/elizabeth-i-build-spanish-armada-1588

History.com Editors. (2009, November 9). Florence Nightingale. History.com; A&E Television Networks. https://www.history.com/topics/womens-history/florence-nightingale-1

History.com Editors. (2009, November 9). John Locke. HISTORY. https://www.history.com/topics/european-history/john-locke

History.com Editors. (2019, June 7). William Shakespeare – Plays, Biography & Poems. History.com. https://www.history.com/topics/european-history/william-shakespeare

History.com Editors. (2019, June 7). Winston Churchill. HISTORY. https://www.history.com/topics/european-history/winston-churchill

History.com Editors. (2023, April 25). Queen Elizabeth II – Childhood, Coronation, Death. HISTORY. https://www.history.com/topics/european-history/queen-elizabeth#a-modern-monarchy

Johnson Lewis, J. (2019, July 21). Biography of Florence Nightingale, Nursing Pioneer. ThoughtCo. https://www.thoughtco.com/about-florence-nightingale-3529854

McNamara, R. (2019, June 18). Biography of Charles Dickens, English Novelist. ThoughtCo. https://www.thoughtco.com/biography-of-charles-dickens-1773689

Pettinger, T. (2012, January 12). William Wilberforce Biography. Biography Online. https://www.biographyonline.net/politicians/uk/william-wilberforce.html

Research, C. E. (2022, October 4). Queen Elizabeth II Fast Facts. CNN. https://edition.cnn.com/2012/12/17/world/europe/queen-elizabeth-ii---fast-facts/index.html

Image Sources

1 https://commons.wikimedia.org/wiki/File:Siege-alesia-vercingetorix-jules-cesar.jpg

2 https://commons.wikimedia.org/wiki/File:King_William_I_(%27The_
Conqueror%27)_from_NPG.jpg

3 https://commons.wikimedia.org/wiki/File:Henry_II_of_England.png

4 https://commons.wikimedia.org/wiki/File:Enrique_VIII_de_Inglaterra,_por_
Hans_Holbein_el_Joven.jpg

5 https://commons.wikimedia.org/wiki/File:Collier%27s_Becket,_Thomas_%
C3%A0.png

6 https://commons.wikimedia.org/wiki/File:Catherine_of_Aragon_(1485-1536).jpg

7 https://commons.wikimedia.org/wiki/File:Elizabeth1England.jpg

8 https://commons.wikimedia.org/wiki/File:Sir_Francis_Walsingham_by_John_
De_Critz_the_Elder.jpg

9 https://commons.wikimedia.org/wiki/File:Gheeraerts_Francis_Drake_1591
_(cropped).jpg

10 https://commons.wikimedia.org/wiki/File:Marlowe-Portrait-1585.jpg

11 https://commons.wikimedia.org/wiki/File:Shakespeare.jpg

12 See page for author, CC BY 4.0 <https://creativecommons.org/licenses/by/4.0>, via
Wikimedia Commons. https://commons.wikimedia.org/wiki/File:
The_Devil_and_Dr._Faustus_meet._Wellcome_L0031469.jpg

13 https://commons.wikimedia.org/wiki/File:Galileo.arp.300pix.jpg

14 https://commons.wikimedia.org/wiki/File:GodfreyKneller-IsaacNewton-1689.jpg

15 https://commons.wikimedia.org/wiki/File:Portrait_of_a_Mathematician_1680c.jpg

16 https://commons.wikimedia.org/wiki/File:Salon_de_Madame_Geoffrin.jpg

17 https://commons.wikimedia.org/wiki/File:JohnLocke.png

18 https://commons.wikimedia.org/wiki/File:William_wilberforce.jpg

19 https://commons.wikimedia.org/wiki/File:William_Bell_Scott_-_Iron_and_Coal.jpg

20 https://commons.wikimedia.org/wiki/File:James_Watt_by_Henry_Howard.jpg

21 https://commons.wikimedia.org/wiki/File:GeorgeStephenson.PNG

22 https://commons.wikimedia.org/wiki/File:Queen_Victoria_-_Winterhalter_1859.jpg

23 https://commons.wikimedia.org/wiki/File:Dickens_Gurney_head.jpg

24 https://commons.wikimedia.org/wiki/File:Florence_Nightingale_CDV_by_H_Lenthall.jpg

25 https://commons.wikimedia.org/wiki/File:Sir_Winston_S_Churchill.jpg

26 https://commons.wikimedia.org/wiki/File:Clementine_Churchill_1915.jpg

27 Luke McKernan, CC BY-SA 2.0 <https://creativecommons.org/licenses/by-sa/2.0>, via Wikimedia Commons. https://commons.wikimedia.org/wiki/File:Battle_of_Britain_(32153121512).jpg

28 https://commons.wikimedia.org/wiki/File:Queen_Elizabeth_II_official_portrait_for_1959_tour_(retouched)_(cropped)_(3-to-4_aspect_ratio).jpg

29 https://commons.wikimedia.org/wiki/File:Charles_and_Diana_1985.JPG

30 https://commons.wikimedia.org/wiki/File:Beatles_ad_1965_just_the_beatles_crop.jpg

www.ingramcontent.com/pod-product-compliance
Lightning Source LLC
Chambersburg PA
CBHW061608120626
46550CB00004B/1650